THE FAST BOWLER'S
BIBLE

Ian Pont

THE FAST BOWLER'S
BIBLE

Ian Pont

THE CROWOOD PRESS

First published in 2006 by
The Crowood Press Ltd
Ramsbury, Marlborough
Wiltshire SN8 2HR

www.crowood.com

This impression 2014

British Library Cataloguing-in-Publication Data
A catalogue record for this book is available from the British Library.

ISBN   1 86126 851 3
EAN   978 1 86126 851 8   *L239,375*

Disclaimer
Whilst every effort has been made to ensure that this book is
technically accurate and sound, neither the author nor the publisher
can accept responsibility for any injury or loss sustained as a result of
using this material. Since the physical activities described in this book
may be too strenuous in nature for some readers to engage in safely,
it is essential that a doctor be consulted prior to undertaking training
and, or, bowling.

Throughout this book 'he', 'him' and his', etc, are used as neutral pronouns
and as such refer to both males and females.

Photographs © Chris Mercer

Typeset in Galliard by Bookcraft Ltd, Stroud, Gloucestershire

Printed and bound in India by Replika Press Pvt. Ltd.

Contents

Acknowledgements

My special thanks for all their help in making this book possible to:

Dr Asaf Bashir (medical, injury prevention and exercises)
Dr Rabi Mehta (sports aerodynamics consultant)
Chris Mercer (sports photographs)
Graham Napier (bowling model)
Antonio Palladino (contribution)
Andrew McGarry (contribution)
Club Woodham Health & Fitness (exercises)
Warsop Stebbing (cricket balls)

Mention must be made of the Philadelphia Phillies baseball team coaching staff for their encouragement and support in initially teaching the mechanics of accuracy and speed together. This was a pivotal discovery for me.

Finally and most importantly, I would like to thank Dr Kenneth L. West personally for his insight, wisdom and collaboration on vital aspects of my own fast bowling coaching methodology. Without his supreme understanding of advanced biomechanics, much of this book could not have been written.

The coaching methods in this book are known as ABSAT (Advanced Biomechanics, Speed and Accuracy Training). ABSAT coaching is a style and methodology designed by the author to give improvements to bowlers in the fastest time, and in a safe way.

absat

For private coaching, individual coaching or to enquire about the 60-beats-per-minute music, please visit www.maverickscricket.com where you will find a contact address, number and email.

Foreword

Quick bowling is the most individual talent in cricket. That's why, if I had to give one piece of advice to a young lad aching to become a fast bowler, it would be 'Do what feels good'. I know it's not the most technical advice in the world, but if your body does not feel comfortable with what you ask it to do, your chances of doing the business will not be very high.

Understanding the basic action is important, but once that has been established just concentrate on accelerating through your run-up, hitting the crease at speed, and propelling that ball as fast as you can. It will soon become clear whether you have the raw materials to become a fast bowler. In the current era, Brett Lee adopts a great position. Biomechanically, the Australian has the perfect action.

Every great fast bowler is different. For every one like Dennis Lillee, another man blessed with a great classical action, there is someone else who is much more unorthodox. Jeff Thomson, Lillee's hunting partner in the great Australian side of the seventies, favoured a slinging action that nobody would ever have tried to coach into him. But Thomson was one of the fastest bowlers in history and, at his peak, terrorised nearly every batsman who faced him.

Just look at the differences in styles. The West Indians, Joel Garner and Curtly Ambrose, gained much advantage from their height. Malcolm Marshall scuttled through the crease at breakneck speed. Colin Croft rocked wide of the crease with an awkward splayfooted action. Yet all were born with the same talent: the ability to propel a cricket ball at speeds around 90mph.

The problem for a teenage fast bowler is that once he gets to a certain age he is surrounded by coaches telling him to change that, and do this, rather than just let him bowl. A lot of coaches try to turn every fast bowler into Richard Hadlee, the essence of a master craftsman, rather than just let them enjoy the game and thrill in their particular blessing.

Often, bowlers without a classical action, who are persuaded by coaches to learn the error of their ways, break down with knee and back problems. Would these injuries have surfaced had they been left alone? In some cases, perhaps they would. But in other cases they break down because they are trying to do something that doesn't come naturally to them.

Refuse the extra net session if you feel too exhausted. Don't always agree to drop your pace and become net fodder. Beware of too many indoor sessions, especially in inferior sports centres, where the jarring on the knee and back can do damage. Concentrate on *quality*, not quantity. Above all, build up your hunger.

Develop a training programme, but only after taking advice from the professionals. Sit-ups done badly, for instance, can do more harm than good – they are less likely to strengthen your abdominal muscles than wreck your back.

Above all, don't bowl through niggling injuries. Get proper advice and get it early. You have only one body. Treat it with the respect it deserves.

I'm a great believer in leaving young bowlers to develop naturally as much as possible. There are great dangers in trying to radically change a natural action that has been functioning perfectly into one that is textbook perfect.

You can always refine an action to gain extra efficiency, but coaches these days are increasingly wary of changing things too much. If a bowler has a special skill at fourteen, there is an argument for leaving that talent well alone. Many promising bowlers have suddenly lost everything and eventually given up the game. Altered actions can look wooden and manufactured.

Budding seam bowlers should remember that they are still growing, and that they should not put their bodies under too much strain for fear of prolonged injury. Over bowling is a problem for many youngsters as they try to balance demands by different clubs, schools and age-group sides. Set yourself a limit.

It is important for a bowler to take advice primarily from one or maybe two people. Find someone who you feel happy with and stick with him. Particularly when you are just starting out, it's a mistake to collect conflicting advice from every different source and then try to stick it all together. That is just a recipe for confusion.

Since my knee injuries I have worked on biomechanics with Steve Oldham at Yorkshire and now Ian Pont at Essex. The reasoning behind this has been to try to be a little more open in my action in terms of getting my front arm to move in the same direction as I am running. All of this work is designed to generate that extra yard of pace that all fast bowlers need to trouble the world's top batsmen.

By now, most people know my attitude. However you spend your life, you might as well try to enjoy it. I'm lucky to play cricket for England, something that millions have dreamed of apart from me, so the least I can do is go about things with a smile on my face.

There is a theory that talented young cricketers don't get the chance to learn to love the game these days. The minute they show any promise, they are packaged off into representative sides, and from there into county nets or cricket academies. Coaching begins at an increasingly early age. In no time, sport has become an examination subject more than a recreation.

Fortunately, I managed to cram in a couple of years at Monk Bretton, in the Pontefract section of the Yorkshire Council, before I started on the treadmill, so I sampled the love for the game that thousands of amateur players at small clubs have. Cricket takes many hours to reach a conclusion, which leaves plenty of time for laughter amid the competition. Every young player should enjoy that humour. Try your utmost while you are on the field, and examine every way to improve your game, but when it's over, try to laugh at both success and failure. That will make your experience so much more worthwhile.

Good luck and keep trying.

Darren Gough

Introduction

I'd like to start by saying that I wish I'd met Ian Pont, the bowling coach, ten years before I did.

Throughout my bowling career I was regarded as a genuine medium pace bowler, who relied on accuracy and swing if the conditions were right. What Ian did for me personally was to make sure that the biomechanics of my action were increased to the maximum to allow me to gain an extra yard of pace.

Biomechanically my action had never been worked on or even modified by coaches throughout my professional career, and those bowlers that were at a higher level than me pacewise always had naturally good biomechanical actions. I was not one of them.

The work I did with Ian helped me rectify this, even though my old action was very much set in its ways. What he did for me was to increase my pace a little bit and got my body and timing working together at point of delivery, thereby increasing my accuracy to a higher level than before. Hence my recall back into the England cricket team 2002, after a break of six years.

Ian Pont is an expert in his field and has some excellent ideas on how to engineer a bowling action. He really highlights the basis of great bowlers of the past and, I hope, the future too.

Yours in cricket
Ronnie Irani

How to Use this Book

I love proverbs and sayings. They can be profound. The Chinese have a great one about learning, which is, 'When the pupil is ready, the teacher will appear'.

So I am going to assume you are ready, because this book is your teacher and the way to use it is to read it and then re-read the relevant sections. Make notes if you wish. But most of all, take time to *understand* what is being said. I don't know what level you are already at, but I do know that the majority of what's in these pages will be new to you.

Having coached at all levels I can honestly say that bowlers learn faster when they challenge what they are doing and interact with the information they are receiving. By that I mean don't merely accept it. Go out and experience it for yourself. Also take time to look at other bowlers and assess their actions, based on the knowledge you will gather from here. This makes you a bowling coach and helps you use a critical eye to consider what's happening in the bowling action. It all helps reinforce your *own* awareness and appreciation too.

I suggest you sit down and read this book through from start to finish. Then go back to Chapter 4 and the section on advanced biomechanics, starting with 'The Keys To Success', taking in each of the points and associated examples, one by one. That's how I would do it the first time out.

Hopefully, you'll find it an interesting read. I suspect you'll find it challenging, which is the point of any good coaching book. It's written in a chatty style, not a stuffy, condescending style that is lecturing. View this book as a friend and mentor. And like all good mates, it will even get the first round of drinks in.

CHAPTER 1

What's Wrong with Coaching?

Over-coaching is as bad as under-coaching. However, I prefer to say that neither of these is the culprit. The *wrong* coaching is the worst of all. Sure, you can coach a young bowler way too much and stifle his natural talent. Equally, there are fast bowlers who are allowed to develop with mistakes in actions that can lead to stress fractures of the spine and other horrendous problems. But the biggest mistake a coach can make is simply giving the wrong information.

The challenge for a coach therefore is to understand how to get the best out of a bowler as well as when to coach and what to coach. This is what makes a coach truly great. But having the knowledge about the bowling action in the first place is paramount. That's why the *MCC Coaching Book* always fascinated me. The bowling section in the book that I used to read and re-read as a child only covered how to bowl with a sideways action. It simply didn't cater for mixed or front-on actions. In fact, it only ever went as far as proposing there is one way to bowl, which is clearly incorrect. Also, it never explained *why* things happened, or attempted to question 'accepted' wisdom.

The incidences of stress-related impact and twisting injuries on the spine have dramatically increased in modern cricket. This may be a combination of many factors, but it's certainly as a result of better monitoring. We have technological advances that can identify and correct injuries and indeed predict if a bowler is likely to have injury problems ahead of them happening. These advances are helping bowlers to understand the limitations of their current bowling action and make biomechanical changes to improve.

But injury prevention is only half of the equation. Increasing a bowler's speed and accuracy is the other side of the coin that has not been fully understood or absorbed. It's good to see changes to coaching courses as biomechanics coaching becomes a more important area that requires better understanding. But we're still a very long way off. That's why this book is for all those who think you cannot help bowlers bowl faster. I've met many of them. I hear coaches and non-coaches, who simply don't know what they're doing, saying just that. I've spoken to officials inside cricket, ex-players and even those running cricket at various levels who have a very old-fashioned view about bowling. It takes time for these people to come to terms with new ideas. It takes even longer for them to change – despite progress being inevitable. All it means is that the rate of success varies widely from country to country, county to county, and club to club.

But all sport moves on and cricket is no exception. For example, the training methods of athletes thirty years ago would be laughable today and every world athletics record has been broken many times. Roger Bannister's world-beating time wouldn't get him within half a lap of the record today. Yet it was hailed as a human triumph in its day, which it was of course. Advances in just about everything, including coaching, have far surpassed what's gone before.

So this isn't about being ungracious to a generation of cricket coaches. But the fact is it's sometimes not easy to accept breakthroughs in coaching methods, simply because they aren't from yesteryear. Either that, or those methods weren't based on what that coach did himself as a player (most coaches coach from playing experience rather than from best practice). This is exactly why the challenge for a fast bowler today is to get access to all relevant information and make his *own* mind up.

That's not a *modern* way of coaching – it's the *only* way of coaching.

A bowler is today almost self-taught or at least 'self-understood', with the coach as a facilitator and guide. It's something coaches are becoming increasingly aware of. Yet as long ago as the early 1970s this truth about fast bowling was taking shape.

At that time a young inexperienced Pakistani bowler called Imran Khan played for Worcestershire in the English County Championship. He bowled little, medium-pace swingers. It was all fairly innocuous stuff. Within eighteen months Imran had developed into one of the world's most devastating bowlers with the skill to bowl in excess of 90mph and swing the ball in late. It was

> Cricket is all about speed these days. Fast bowling, fast spin and fast batting. That means the speed of the ball, bat speed and the speed of revolutions on the ball. That's why I felt if we had four bowlers bowling over 85mph we had a chance of winning the Ashes.
>
> Duncan Fletcher

a complete transformation. No one who had seen him at the start could have imagined the changes one person could make in such a short space of time.

So what was his secret? His action. He changed it. He worked on his delivery and ability to get the most out of his body at the crease to get the ball swinging at pace. The results were miraculous. Of course, he also worked on his fitness and strength too. And these served to support his new action perfectly. Imran was one of the first to truly adopt biomechanics in its truest sense.

What's more, as a great attacking batsman he went on to become one of the best all-round cricketers of all time. But he will always be remembered for his wonderful action and tremendous ability to destroy batting line-ups with the ball.

So take heart – whatever level you're at you can improve what you've got. All you need to know is *how* to do it.

CHAPTER 2

One for the Ladies

It shouldn't be overlooked that the England Ladies' Test Team *also* won the Ashes in 2005. That was a magnificent achievement and credit goes to all the players and support staff for making it happen. Ladies' cricket generally is moving in the right direction and it's being taken more seriously by administrators, which is great news. Sadly though, ladies' cricket suffers from a lack of funding. And that's not surprising, given the poor media coverage it has to put up with.

However, with specific reference to coaching, this book applies equally to male *and* female fast bowlers. I do not distinguish between the two for purposes of learning. But I do make an apology.

I refer throughout this book to 'he' rather than 'she' when describing the bowler. This is purely because it would be tedious to write 'he/she' every time and it breaks up the enjoyment of reading. So I ask all female cricketers to bear with me on this point. It's not designed to exclude – merely to aid the pleasure of reading the secrets revealed.

As an aside, I look forward to working with the England Ladies' Team very soon. And I'm hoping that up-and-coming girls, as well as newcomers to female cricket, can absorb the information just as well as their male counterparts. I would imagine in many cases even more so.

Apart from the obvious physical differences, there is no reason why women can't improve just as quickly. In fact, I still hope we see the world's first 80mph female fast bowler sometime soon. The right person equipped physically to do it and with the knowledge found here, could take the female game by storm.

Watch this space.

CHAPTER 3

Blowing the Lid off Fast Bowling

February in Port Elizabeth, South Africa

It's called the Windy City. But for now it's calm, *shimmeringly* hot and very, very sunny. Azure blue skies, the beach and the Indian Ocean make this an attractive seaside resort, offering far too many distractions as the build up to the Cricket World Cup begins.

If only cricket was played in England in weather like this. We'd be world-beaters. But our weather is not so good.

I have heard pundits and coaches say that's partially the reason we don't have hoards of fast bowlers queuing up. That and, of course, the consequently slow pitches. They must be to blame. It's always cold, damp or unsavoury conditions that affect our quickies. How can you encourage bowlers to bowl fast when it's like that?

We use this at least in part to explain why, after many years of trying, we have not had a fast bowling attack to fear over a long period of time. Don't get me wrong. Now and again we produce the *odd* quickie. And if we're really lucky, two or three might be around at the same time. And when this happens our Test cricket team suddenly starts doing well. Funny that, isn't it? But if one or two get injured or lose form, we're back to square one again.

One can only imagine, then, how wonderful English cricket would be if we played it in warm sunshine all the time. After all, the weather is responsible. Isn't it?

Here's why it's *not*.

Looking back over my cricket career I can honestly say that not one coach actually showed me *how* to bowl fast. It's an area we should be expert in. But to do this requires *understanding* rather than regurgitation of facts.

A young bowler who wants to know *how* to bowl fast or to learn the skills of what it takes to become a truly fast bowler will find that these skills are not widely taught. And for me, I was left with a coach (usually ex-professional) trying to get me to bowl how they bowled. If it didn't work, they'd feel comforted by the fact that 'fast bowlers are born, not made'. (The opposite of that is the truth, and this book will help explain why.) What they in fact meant was, *raw talent* is born. You can make the best out of anything if you know what to do. And that's the secret.

Equally as important, no one explained *why* they were coaching what they were coaching. The simple truth may have been, and possibly still is, that they didn't know either.

I recall spending a winter whilst teaching sport at Stowe School. I was twenty-one years old. The previous summer, Nottinghamshire had released me after being signed as an all-rounder on a two-year contract. Bob White, the 2nd XI coach at Notts at the time, suggested that I try to become a fast bowler rather than a steady seamer. So that winter at Stowe, I shed two stone in weight and used my spare time to work out building up my back and shoulder muscles. The results were dramatic.

It was a watershed for me because I discovered two things that would change the way I viewed fast bowling. The first was that you have to *want* to bowl fast. The second was that no one around was going to be able to help. This, without question, would be a journey of self-discovery.

Almost by accident I realised it was possible to increase speed and accuracy by stretching and contracting certain muscles groups, and by getting the body into specific positions. Not only did this improve bowling but also throwing, a fact I was to put to the test in America on tryouts as a baseball pitcher with the New York Yankees. Spurred on by great results I went back to America for six weeks and spent the spring training with the Philadelphia Phillies where I learnt the facts about advanced biomechanics.

However it wasn't until some nine years later in 1996 that I met Dr Ken West, a professor of biomechanics who was able to reveal the *why* part of bowling fast. He not only confirmed what I had discovered for myself but also proved that *anyone* can improve speed and accuracy by positioning. This was very exhilarating.

Working alongside Ken has given me the tools to explain the *how to* part of fast bowling in a way that is easy to understand and more importantly, can be replicated.

Any good sports coach seeking credibility should be able to explain the *why* and *how to* part of what they are saying. In other words, understand what the body does and help the student to *feel* their body working in that way. It is only by challenging that we ultimately discover.

The fact is, cricket coaching is usually performed by the generation before, who in turn were taught by the generation before them.

Fathers tend to coach sons and pass on their knowledge from their own experiences and what they were told. Older club players coach youngsters the same way.

It means many beliefs and phrases have become 'accepted' as the norm being passed from grandfather to father to son but were not always explained – just copied. Think of all those generations passing on things they hadn't really questioned? Like why do we coach a certain way, or where's the proof something works? It's only very recently that the side-on action has been queried. Indeed, many current coaches still say that getting side-on in the action is the *only* way to show and coach a young fast bowler, which of course is clearly wrong.

Yet year after year we see an alarming prevalence of back injuries and career-threatening stress fractures. More bowlers are having their actions remodelled and reshaped by coaches like National Academy Fast Bowling Coach Troy Cooley and myself. Cricket coaching has evolved into as much about *preventing* injury as being able to bowl well, because it's sometimes too late trying to help someone after they've been badly injured. I am in the camp that says let's get a bowler bowling naturally, with an action they feel happy with, but within certain boundaries or guidelines. You have to have an action that's robust, supportive and above all as stress-free as possible, bearing in mind that fast bowling is very hard work. And when you achieve this, you automatically find it easier to be consistent with your action and duplicate the same delivery. Plus of course, you have more chance of bowling faster and in a straight line. That's why Troy's work at the ECB (England and Wales Cricket Board) has been as important for preventing injury as mine is for increasing pace and accuracy.

It's the very reason – when it comes to the history of coaching – why we need to be selective about the information we choose to give people. A coach needs to be flexible, adaptive and understanding of the bowling action.

Because any good methodology should stand up to close scrutiny, or at least be responsible for some measure of success and excellence. Excellence isn't just a word (even though we hear it bandied around as though it is). To *truly* achieve excellence, one must have opened the mind to all possibilities and then chosen the best route.

Clearly, this has not been the case with fast bowling in England over the years. But that's all changing dramatically. The England team has won the Ashes back after eighteen years. And guess what? We out-bowled the Australian attack comfortably. Yes that's right. With some excellent fast bowling and reverse swing, the English bowlers came out on top. It didn't just happen overnight. The success had been planned some five years earlier, and a strategy identified. Thanks to a combination of many factors coming together, England out-played Australia.

Understanding of the bowling action is an integral part of improvement. Now discover the secrets of what's involved. Read for yourself the facts about pace, accuracy and how to make the most of your own bowling.

I am a firm believer in utilising your natural talent as best you can. You can do this by choosing the best bits of advice in this book and trying them out. If they feel right then they probably are right – for you. At the end of the day you must feel 100 per cent behind any changes you make, otherwise don't bother. It's no good being half-hearted about things. Get a plan of your own and put it in place.

I hope this book helps you to introduce new ideas and ways to coach, which in turn can refresh and inspire those you choose to help – or help yourself. At the very worst, you'll be making a real difference to the lives of many cricketers and your own.

If the book is purely for your own game, then the truth is you now hold the future in your hands. That means it's time to get excited.

CHAPTER 4

Fast Bowling Coaching Made Easy

Tell me and I will forget. Show me and I will remember. Involve me and I will understand.

Benjamin Franklin

To coach or not to coach, that is the question. Do you leave raw talent alone or do you interfere with it? And if so, when is the best time to coach?

The problem is, someone with raw, genuine talent may have a technically unsound action or, at least, an unusual way of delivering the ball. There would be an overwhelming temptation to correct it. Let's take Shaun Tait of Australia as an example.

Fast bowler Tait took more Pura Cup wickets in the 2004–2005 Australian domestic season than anyone else. That might be because he bowled really well. Or it might be because it summed up the standard of Australian domestic batting. Either way it got him selected for the Ashes squad. Yet his action is *riddled* with challenges from a biomechanical point of view. I am being polite. He does many things wrong and some of them are working against him in his quest to have a long career.

Yes it's true he can get the ball out of his hand at around 90mph. And that's why the general view is he should be left alone to bowl as he wants. So I can see why this 'non-intervention' option would be very appealing. However, despite appearing as though change would be difficult, it could be done. The results, I think, would be spectacular and he could enjoy startling success with greater pace, accuracy and straight lines. Perhaps the changes ought to have been made in development as a junior, although some coaches will say maybe not.

Another player who had some issues with his bowling was Jason Gillespie. But his situation is completely different. Two seasons prior to the 2005 Ashes summer, Gillespie was one of the world's leading fast bowlers. He had pace, movement and bounce. This meant he troubled even the best of the batsmen he came up against. Yet in 2005 I watched this giant of a man visibly wilt under the pressure of inconsistency. His Ashes summer fell apart. And the dreadful thing was that no one seemed to know how to correct it, least of all the bowler himself. With approximately fifty differing pieces of (incorrect) advice ringing in his ears, I can imagine the poor guy was the most confused man on the planet as everyone rallied to tell him what he was doing wrong.

The sad thing is his remedy was quite simple, and covers two of the fast bowling keys mentioned later (chest drive and exit stride). Gillespie has the type of action where he needs momentum to get out of the crease. He has fast arms and a big rotation. That's why, when he doesn't bowl particularly well, it's because he gets 'stuck' in the crease and doesn't get out of it. The solution is *not* to run in harder or faster, as I heard he had been told to do. His 'bouncy' run-up is for rhythm, not ground-speed rhythm like Lee or Akhtar. It would seem that Gillespie's solution is a very personal thing, and should take place under the watchful eye and help of a knowledgeable coach. This will also help build confidence, which is another attribute of a good tutor.

So, generally, at what point is bowling coaching the right thing to do? My own personal view is that sharing of information is the key. By having all the knowledge available, a player can choose what they want to do. After all, it is the bowler who has to buy into it.

That's why a coach's knowledge of fast bowling dictates how well he can help others. And that's why this book gives you the ammunition to make the right decisions.

Bowling coaching is made up of many things. Understanding the action is an *integral* part. Knowing how to avoid injury and keep a stable position at delivery is another. But when you think of bowling coaching, you also think of line and length, swing and seam, accuracy and bowling in the right 'areas'. So let's be honest here, none of that has changed.

'Traditional' coaching still holds good today. Indeed, some argue that we've moved too far away from those values. And I agree. Bowlers seem to spend less time bowling at targets, learning how to move the ball or knowing which type of delivery to bowl, and when. Equally, unless their bowling actions have reliability, they cannot reproduce results again and again, since bowling, by nature, is a repetitive business.

So what *is* exciting is the blending together of all that knowledge – and the use of coaching in 'bite-sized' pieces. Plus, of course, being positive. It's really easy to find faults with bowlers when they are not performing. It's human nature to be critical, to be cynical, to have a 'half-empty glass' approach. However, great coaches have to understand human behaviour too. They need to be optimistic, generous in praise and, above all, upbeat and enthusiastic.

Over the years I have come across coaches who do none of this. They are negative, downbeat, always looking for reasons why someone will fail. This, of course, is a recipe for disaster, with either the player or coach (or both) failing miserably to produce the goods. This book is an exciting and vibrant manual with a 'can do' attitude. And just before you get into it, here's one piece of advice. I'd like you to experiment and exaggerate. By that I mean when you practice you should experiment and exaggerate so you experience changes. Never be afraid to change. Never be afraid to question what you do. (In fact always question what you do – it helps you understand.)

The golfer Tiger Woods works on his golf swing pretty much all the time. In his highly technical sport making key adjustments to become consistent are crucial for success. Yet in cricket we've tended to avoid practising those very skills we seek to improve. So get out there and practise. Try it out. Make mistakes. Because it's only by making mistakes and discovering our limitations that we truly learn. Make as many mistakes as you like, just don't keep making the same ones.

THE KEYS TO SUCCESS

It is very important to discover as early on as possible the *keys to success* that will help you bowl faster and straighter. When you understand them you will realise just how it is possible to improve both pace and accuracy at the same time.

This is an important point. In fact, it's so profound that it's worth repeating: it is possible to improve both pace and accuracy at the same time.

Due to the way we coach and the beliefs we hold so dear, it is thought that speed and

I did not bowl a lot when I was young and I think that sort of helped me. How you look after yourself is very important off the field. I train quite hard in the gym and look to build my strength and flexibility up. The other one is to have a very good action. I have been lucky that I have a very stress-free action. I am quite front-on and tend to go through the crease using my side muscles and stomach muscles more than my back muscles, and that puts me in good stead. If you have a very good action and work well off the field then you will be fine.

Glenn McGrath

accuracy cannot go together. Let me dispel that theory, because if this were really true then the slower you bowled the more accurate you'd be. And we'd all be bowling slower balls all the time. So let's not confuse bowlers who are 'trying to bowl too fast' with incorrect mechanics. If the ball comes out badly or inaccurately, chances are the mechanics are wrong. And these can be put right.

One of the most common coaching phrases to a wayward young quickie is 'slow down son, bowl a line and length.' Every coach reading this book who has uttered those infamous words to a young speedster is responsible for potentially shattering the dreams of another hopeful. That's because the most important element to becoming a fast bowler is *desire*.

So I want to look at this the other way round. Embrace the young bowler who tries to bowl fast, wants to bowl fast, and likes to bowl fast – and explain to him *how* to bowl fast. Desire is something that you cannot teach. So why snuff it out by stopping him from trying to bowl fast? Rather, *help him to perform the mechanics correctly from the start*, and watch him grow into a special talent.

When you understand what's going on in the bowling action from a technical point of view, you've got half a chance. The line and length is simply a *result* of the action. So focusing on the cause is the answer. Otherwise, all you're asking a bowler to do is compensate and make allowances for incorrect biomechanics. The bowler will then either evolve with a problem action or, worse still, never be able to bowl truly fast.

Let's get the biomechanics right first. The rest will follow. This will give youngsters the best chance of success. Personally, I would rather see a young fast bowler trying to bowl *too* fast. I feel that more inaccuracy comes from bowling slower balls than faster ones.

I recall a conversation with the great Middlesex and West Indies paceman, Wayne Daniel. On hearing that I had been told to concentrate on trying to hit the seam and shape the ball better when I bowled, he remarked 'Man, just bowl at 100mph and let the batsman *negotiate* the ball.' Whilst it may have been a throwaway comment, the underlying principle of great West Indian fast bowling during the 1980s was revealed in all its glory right there. The message was: bowl as fast as you can, then worry about where it goes later. That appealed to me because I had the desire to bowl fast in the first place. In England we teach accuracy, line and length before we come to pace.

Interestingly, both schools of thought have merits and flaws. The reason is that you can have speed *and* accuracy. One is not at the expense of the other. This is probably the most important discovery for seam bowling for a generation. By perfecting your mechanics to the point that you can maximise speed, you also give yourself the best set of tools for accuracy too. That's because the tools are ultimately the same.

Of course there are *fast* bowlers and there are fast bowlers. Truly quick bowlers are not fazed by pitch conditions because of their natural speed through the air. These guys can rip out a batting order – particularly the tail – to win matches on batting-friendly tracks.

From a personal viewpoint I feel there is far too much emphasis by coaches on getting bowlers to move the ball large amounts. A ball only has to deviate two inches to miss the middle of the bat and take the edge – any more than this is a waste.

There's talk of bowling in 'good areas' and getting 'good shape' to the ball. (Actually there is only *one* area.) But this is a book that teaches you how to be as accurate as you want and as fast as you can. This book will also touch on the wrist positions you need to use to achieve the 'shape' of the ball. But for now that's peripheral stuff. We want to be producing fast bowlers with the ability to make a difference.

I'd like to see a return to a fast bowling attack that scares the opposition before they take the field. It's probably worth a couple of wickets. Let's face it, lightning speed yorkers and chest height rearing deliveries are extremely hard to play. The greatest sides over the years have all had one or two genuinely quick bowlers and the poorer sides have not. For me, the paceman remains king of the crop – particularly when one realises that accuracy *does not* have to suffer.

If you doubt this, think about a bowling attack trying to take twenty wickets every game to win the match. Unless the pitch is turning square or it is a minefield, the chances are it's going to be the new-ball bowlers who have a great deal of sway. Getting the right start with a new ball is vitally important. And those teams that do not have a 'gun' attack or at least one excellent new-ball bowler can find it very hard to compete all season.

My belief is that without at least one genuine speedster in a team, any side lacks the cutting edge to be consistently good.

Sadly, for my own career, the amazing discovery of teaching biomechanics for fast bowlers came too late. I had received coaching from well-known names that had been international bowlers (no names mentioned), but they didn't know how to teach me *how to*. Nor could they explain it. Unsurprisingly, all they had me do was bowl like they did. Which of course worked for them. But that's not always the best way to coach. I can understand why coaches do it though. They're basing it on their own experiences and their own limitations. And if they've been a great player, it seems the easiest thing in the world to pass on what they did as gospel.

This is cloning at it's very worst, because it makes no allowance for the individual. I'm not talking about the strategic stuff of where to bowl (we all know what we *should* be doing), I am talking about improving base actions, straight lines and speed.

One particular session set me back months after I lengthened my run-up, changed my delivery stride and spent hours doing the wrong things. It was confusing and almost a devastating mistake.

The trouble is, we all put store in someone's ability to coach *just* because they may have been a great player. It's difficult for a player to question a coach – particularly if that coach used to be well known, well respected or a giant on the playing field. Yet the truly great coaches should always welcome being challenged. The best teachers will interact and understand the student's thinking. A coach's job is to impart the right knowledge for the student in a way that's best absorbed.

Let's be brutal here. Current bowling coaching largely consists of babysitting sessions. Not much real coaching goes on – if any. I would go so far as to say that it is largely overlooked. Bowlers are allowed to carry on with errors they find hard to correct. But without intervention, improvements take far longer. And the bowler doesn't develop properly, or simply remains at medium pace, trying to compensate for lack of speed by swing and seam. If they do develop their speed, it's more by luck than by how much they've learned.

It means there's far more to coaching fast bowling than standing at the end of the net shouting 'Well bowled', 'Great areas', or 'There's good shape on that'. The reality is that 99 percent of bowlers already know if they've bowled a good ball or a bad one. The bowler understands that the long hop he's just been hit for four with wasn't very smart. He knows that the inswinging leg-cutter that hit the top off-stump was a delivery that was unplayable.

What he needs to know is how to replicate the great deliveries time after time – and how to avoid bowling the bad ones.

I respect those people who tried to help me. It was just that they didn't understand the *how to* part of fast bowling. At the time of writing this, I know of only one coach in the world actively sharing the secrets of *how to* bowl fast. But that's the exciting part. There is now a way forward. You no longer have to decide whether to choose speed or accuracy. The truth is you *can* have it all.

I am about to share with you the *keys to success* that can make a staggering difference to any bowler. These keys require explaining in great detail, with photographs and demonstrations. So later in the book you'll find headings that greatly simplify the understanding process and visuals to make each point.

But I'll give you an *overview* of the process with these keys first. And whilst these keys are written as bullet points they are, in fact, the secrets of success. They form the basis for all your coaching. You may end up working on your action thinking about something else but you can relate what you're working on to one of these keys.

Get used to them. Understand them. Get familiar with the language. You will not have seen them before. I guarantee it. That's why working with them gives you a huge advantage. Because it's the first time they've been written down and explained in any kind of detail. It's the first time you'll read about the *how to* part of fast bowling, which also answers the *why* part at the same time.

Fast bowling keys:

- The faster the bowling arm comes over, the faster the ball comes out.
- The arm is speeded up by stretching and contracting the correct muscles in the correct sequence.
- Your front foot landing position should be slightly 'open' compared to the back foot.
- At the point of delivery, the bowler should be face on to the batsman (nose and hips).
- The furthest point forward in the bowling action is the chest, followed by the hips.
- The hips drive towards the front knee to create a power blast.
- The chest is tensed forward, whilst the rest of the body is relaxed.
- The drive of the chest and hips provides a 'boomerang' shape to the body, which increases the speed of the arm on delivery.
- The position of the hips provides the power and stability for bowling fast.
- The non-bowling arm is *just* as important as the bowling arm.
- A full and complete 180-degree rotation of both shoulders is vital.
- The bowling shoulder should be 'buried' into the pitch after delivery.
- The non-bowling arm helps pull that side of the body 'out of the way'.
- Travel in straight lines at the batsman.
- Aim to follow-through by about 50 percent of the length of your run-up.

The bullet points above cover 99.9 percent of what a bowler will need to get right. If you look at the world's truly great quick bowlers, you'll see they do most, if not all, of the above. It means you can relate anything you're working on to one of the key points. That's why it's a blueprint and that's why you must understand the process.

But there would be little point in me sharing the process with you if it was overtly technical or you couldn't understand it. That's why this whole area of advanced biomechanics has been largely overlooked or at least avoided and left to technical experts. It's been seen as something hard to appreciate, difficult to get across and tough to comprehend. So I have great faith in you that you'll understand exactly what I'm saying.

I've spent years working with local, school, club, county and international bowlers in an attempt to ensure that the learning method works. It's been perfected so that beginners to fast bowling, as well as those at the top of world cricket, can improve through the techniques used here.

As you go through this book, I'd encourage you to look back at the keys regularly. Because when we go into more detail you'll find the information connects with these keys. You'll have to use the keys to unlock the information you're being given.

When you do this you'll learn faster and your understanding will be deeper. So let's analyse the action in more detail and explain *how to* bowl fast.

Before we start let me just say that we're not building robots here. This is not about *cloning* bowling actions. And any coaches that tell you it is simply don't get it.

If we took a hundred bowlers and asked them all to bowl the same way, they would all look different. It's what we've been doing for many years already. This book is all about 'best practice'. And it's also about giving you the information you need to be a success. So please take the information and use it. Follow the guidance for yourself and try it out. Experiment. Exaggerate. Try to break the mould. Learning is fun.

WHAT ARE ADVANCED BIOMECHANICS?

'Bio' means 'of the body' and 'mechanics' means 'movement'. So we're talking about movement of the body or, more specifically, the bowling action. The advanced part is all about improving the bowling action in a way that's easily understood.

I'm not sure this is anything new. After all, we've been coaching bowling actions for centuries. But what I am certain of is that this is a brand new way of saying it to get results. And what's more, most coaches don't really 'understand' what goes on in a bowling action. When you do realise it, you understand how the bowling action affects your accuracy, speed, chances of injury and ability to be consistent. It also dictates how much stress and strain you put on your body.

In other words, it simply means that the way your body moves through the bowling action affects how fast and straight you bowl. This is the point of this book. The better your body positions itself, the faster and straighter you can become. So advanced biomechanics are about two major things: body position, and muscle stretch and contraction.

When your bowling action is lined up *correctly* and the muscles are stretched and contracted in the right sequence, you bowl at pretty nearly maximum capacity for your physique. And this is what we're trying to achieve. Much of this text is aimed at helping you get into certain positions to allow that to happen.

However, the challenge is in understanding the detail, because up until now that has not been easy. It's the main reason this book even exists. Also I want to expose some myths and introduce you to something fresh and thrilling.

Coaches have been coaching bowling actions the same way for years. And they will continue to do so. The major difference here is that I will give you an understanding of the bowling action in a way you have not known before.

The excitement is in the detail of the action rather than just the action itself. You will have a deeper knowledge of what's working in your bowling action and what you need to put right, because when you get things right you improve. When you know how to get the detail of the action right you'll improve faster. That's why I put a great deal of emphasis on self-awareness for the bowler.

Effective questioning and attentive listening will enable you to get the best from yourself (or any bowler you coach). It is useful to ask effective open questions (of yourself or a student) in a bid to improve performance.

Each of the questions should relate to one of the following elements: thought; feeling; will and action. It would help if you ask yourself:

1. How clear are my *thoughts* about what I want to achieve?
2. To what extent are my *emotions* aligned to that vision?
3. How far am I *committed* to this aim?
4. How advanced is my *action* plan for implementing it?

I don't wish to go into the theories of how you learn, but I do want you to use the information you read here. It's a thought-provoking issue and I want you to really think about the learning process. In other words, don't leave learning to chance. Have some sort of plan for yourself. To do that you must understand the process of fast bowling. To accelerate your learning you will need to understand the action, and appreciate the biomechanics.

What makes the information in this book so easy to access is that it is a clever combination of the learning preferences (kinaesthetic, visual and auditory). I believe you need to *feel* improvements (kinaesthetic) and see how to do it (visual), rather than be *told* about it

(auditory). Traditional coaching tends to be heavily auditory with a coach standing at the end of a net shouting at you (often with a cup of tea in hand).

Understanding the complex area of advanced biomechanics in a simplistic way offers you something new. It offers you the chance to know what you're doing, how to improve and a method for putting things right. What could be better than that?

SUCCESS KEYS EXPLAINED ANOTHER WAY

This is the part where you keep the keys handy and work out which ones relate to which explanation. The keys are at the very heart of understanding your action. I'm going to explain them in other ways to ensure you really get to grips with what I'm talking about.

Sometimes it's easier to comprehend something when it's related to something else. I call it *analogy* coaching and it's my favourite way of helping bowlers appreciate how to achieve a desired effect.

Running and bowling in straight lines

This is a simple concept, yet few actually understand the reasons why they should do it. So let's think about the benefits of running and bowling in straight lines. First, there's less to go wrong. If you're moving in the direction you want to go it helps.

Second, by lining everything up straight you are far more likely to continue on that line unless, of course, you suddenly veer off to one side or the other. This may seem highly logical and obvious and it is. The upside is you have greater momentum, power and control when you are working along a straight line.

Yet you will see bowlers with angled run-ups (virtually all left-arm bowlers have this).

I hear many reasons and theories as to why. I'm afraid that none of them have much logical reasoning. The point is, if you run in a straight line and all your levers move through a straight line, then you follow the ball down the pitch in a straight line, where do you think the ball is most likely to go? You guessed it – in a straight line.

But let's take other sports as examples. Can you imagine a long jumper or a triple jumper with an angled run-up? What would that achieve? Or how about a swimmer starting in lane one and ending up in lane eight? Maybe you've seen a javelin thrower coming in from a 45-degree angle to throw straight? No, it would be nonsense. The simple fact is if you want to bowl straight, you can help yourself by making sure you run along the line you wish

A balanced, straight approach to the crease is desirable to maintain good posture and control.

to bowl. Remember, fast bowling is all about momentum. And it's your ability to keep your momentum moving towards the batsman that helps your speed and accuracy. So ask yourself what you want to do as a fast bowler and what the reasoning is behind it.

Most bowlers who have angled run-ups (or jump in or out at delivery) usually do it to compensate for something else they're not happy with in their action. Or maybe they have the misguided belief that it assists them in some way. However, it just makes it harder to achieve what you want because there is more to go wrong. Bearing in mind we're trying to bowl accurately, consistently and maximising speed, it makes no logic to go round corners to bowl. Maybe I'm exaggerating the point somewhat. But it does impact on balance, feet positioning, lining up of hips and being able to 'get out' of your action on follow through.

Other classic non-straight line issues are bowlers 'falling away' in delivery, shoulders rotating across the body instead of forward, front bowling arms being brought up and back (but not getting forward) and actions leaning back, when we require them to be forward and through towards the batsman.

Of course there will always be examples of bowlers who are very good in spite of having some of these faults. They are not good because they have these faults though. They have merely learned to compensate for them in their actions. What's more, some very awkward actions have led to injury problems, so it is an area you need to consider very carefully. You also may have an action so entrenched in error that you can *only* bowl by angling your run-up. That's why it's for you to choose what you want to do, how far you want to progress and how much you want to take on board in order to improve.

The message is: everything you do is best served in straight lines. In an ideal world you'd choose this. That's because you're targeting the batsman with your entire movement and impetus. In other words, all your momentum is going towards where you want to bowl the ball. Your energy is going where the ball is going and you're about to follow it through.

A martial arts 3rd Dan Black Belt put it succinctly to me when he said 'Imagine your feet and hips are on the two rails of a railway track. Then everything you do goes down that line'.

I would say that's the best way of describing it. After all, trains travel faster on the straight. So do cars, bikes and people. In fact, just about everything does. It means your effort is ultimately going in one direction – at the target. If you consider this it makes perfect sense, but bowlers find numerous reasons for why they angle run-ups and turn their bodies into weird and wonderful positions. Your head is also important here. It's one of the heaviest parts of your body. So it would make sense to keep it going at the batsman in a straight line. It would also help to keep it as still as possible through the action, as it also contains your camera (eyes). Also, it lets the rest of your body know when you are balanced. If you start throwing your head about or have it leaning one way or the other, there's less chance you'll be in control. You will certainly find it harder to focus on where you want to bowl.

With a balanced body position moving through the crease, your action becomes smoother and more effective. And with your head still, you can look at the target.

The truth is that at delivery your hips and nose have to face where the ball is going. Every bowler is in the same position. Why make it hard for yourself? Therefore, if you want to be a fast bowler, pay attention to the line you're moving along.

One other thing. If you're worried about swinging the ball (I hear bowlers say that's why they do things at crazy angles), swing comes from the bowling *wrist position*. A firm, locked wrist swings it out. A soft wrist pushes it in. We'll cover all this in the strategic bowling section later.

So now you don't need to bowl round arm or run in at angles any more.

Run-Up

When I first saw fast bowler Simon Jones of England ambling up off a modest run-up and then hurling the ball at above 90mph (144km/h), I thought 'How does he not hurt himself?'. And I'm glad to see he has increased his run-up. But as a consequence he has dropped his speed. In fact, he lost one of the potential world-class weapons he had. And that's because his mechanics have changed. To compensate, he's learned to reverse swing the ball like a good'un. Some might say he's a far better bowler because of the change. And his statistics confirm that to be true. He was an integral part of England's 2005 Ashes-winning team.

But it does go to prove a point, which is that the *crease* is the most important area when generating speed. This is why Jones could bowl so quickly before and has now dropped his pace down. (If he wanted to he could get back to his original pace and *really* be a handful.)

So run-up is a very personal thing. You should therefore select a run-up that gets you to the crease properly balanced, and in control. If you charge in too fast, it's hard to stretch all the muscles and contract them in time. Amble in too slowly and you can end up stretching for the crease or, worse, not having enough momentum to 'get through' correctly. It is for you to choose what suits your style best.

A word here on run-up speeds. Bowlers with a side-on action tend to run in slower to the crease than bowlers with a front-on action.

The reason is that with a side-on action there has to be time to get the body rotated into a front-on delivery release point. And naturally that doesn't have to happen if the action is *already* front-on. So it simply means the more sideways or square to the batsman you are, the slower you are likely to run in, or want to run in. If you came in too fast with a sideways style of action you'd undoubtedly feel that you couldn't get your action through in time.

This probably explains why some bowlers with certain styles of bowling action prefer to run up a slope rather than down it to bowl. It also means that a run-up is very personal to you. Many factors will dictate the length, angle and speed of your run-up. Ultimately, you'll choose the one to suit your style.

Medium-pacer Angus Fraser had a fast bowler's run-up. He seemed to run *way* too far for the speed he bowled, but of course he relied on 'rhythm'. This suited him and he felt comfortable with it. Part of the reason he had to run this far was because, mechanically, he wasn't quite right. Yet he bowled beautifully for Middlesex and England over many years – he had learned to compensate. Graham Dilley was another bowler who used a lengthy run-up but didn't come charging in from it. Dilley was decidedly fast and his run-up worked very well.

Jason Gillespie has a very 'bouncy' type of run-up. This serves him well for getting his body and feet moving with good rhythm, but he doesn't run in particularly fast, unlike

When you come into bowl in a meaningful way, you will find it helps set the 'tone' of your bowling.

By focusing on your stride pattern you can check that your landing position is going to be correct. This is done with a 'still' head, which keeps your eyes level.

Shoaib Akhtar, Brett Lee or Dale Steyn. These three really attack the crease with lengthy run-ups that are in themselves full of pace. It's interesting to note that they are all capable of bowling at around 95mph (152km/h) and above, making them the three fastest bowlers in the world at present.

This is my point about run-ups. There is no real 'right' way – only *your* way.

However, you should at least run in straight lines. I do despair when coaches force bowlers in off an angled run. Once again, if you have the correct set up at the crease and line up, why would you need to run in at an angle? Only a poor mechanics' coach suggests an angled run. The angle of the run-up has very

little to do with movement of the ball either. Since both swing and seam come from the fingers and wrist position, make sure you get the mechanics right at the crease to support your hand.

The Gather

There's a point at which everything you learn and implement in your bowling action begins. It's the starting place for your action and it sets the scene.

It's called the gather because it's where you 'gather' up your bowling action ready for release. The importance of the gather is that

A final glance at the crease to safeguard you don't overstep. This is part of the 'trigger' so you can relax into your bowling action at take-off stride.

The gather is the start of your delivery sequence. It takes place about two steps from the crease and is a smooth transition from your run-in to bowl.

it acts as one of the most significant triggers, because it's from here you'll try to unleash your action in the crease. And if you are all over the place and not controlled at this point, things will go wrong later.

So think of the gather as one of a series of checkpoints (along with hang time, *see* below), which help you to maintain control over your action. It takes place in the pre-delivery stride and is almost exclusively an upper body and trunk movement. This is a transition from your run-up into your bowling action and marks the beginning of the delivery.

As you run in to bowl, whether it be fast or not, you'll have to set yourself into a bowling position. This movement is where your shoulders and hips begin to take over from your legs and start to 'set' into the bowling action.

Bowlers with a more sideways action will find there's an initial trunk twisting and counter shoulder rotation going on (towards the leg side). The hips also begin to turn at this point, bringing your upper body into a more 'square' attitude relative to the batsman. However, a bowler with a front-on action will find the gather is led by the arms and shoulders coming up rather than by the hips, which should already be front-on in the running style and therefore change little.

The gather is therefore a trigger movement, and it's worth being aware of the correct positioning and control so that you can 'firm up' your bowling action. It's a precursor to what follows.

Hang Time

Following on from, and directly related to, the gather is hang time. But whereas the gather is almost exclusively an upper body and trunk movement, hang time is controlled by the bottom half of your body and legs.

This isn't *strictly* a biomechanics issue but

it does affect your bowling in such a fundamental way that I've included it here. You may need to read this part in the book sequence in which it's written, then return to it once you understand the secrets of your action. This is because it impacts on your ability to utilise your action and make the most of it. In other words, it's a trigger for what is about to follow.

Hang time is something that some bowlers have and others don't. The top fast bowlers all seem to have it, although there are a few notable exceptions. Hang time is the ability to 'hang' in the air just prior to delivery. It comes from being able to get airborne and hold this position while you set yourself to bowl.

This hang time varies from bowler to bowler. Yet, when a bowler is able to 'climb' into a strong holding position they have the

The upper body takes over the action and begins to move the shoulders and hips into place. Note the balanced head position, with the eyes focused on the target.

The right knee (left knee for left-arm bowler) powers upwards and forwards to help get the bowler off the ground. The result is a leap into the air. The upper body is controlled still by the arms and shoulders to ensure everything continues to move forward towards the batsman in a straight line.

With the upper body posture 'set' and the bowler's momentum coming at the batsman, this is a good, relaxed hang time position.

best chance to control their action. So, for me, hang time is about management of your bowling action. But it does depend upon your set up.

Wasim Akram had very little hang time. That's because he had a shuffling, very busy style of run-up. He generated his power and speed from a fast arm. Yet biomechanically he certainly didn't tick all the boxes. Despite this, Akram was a devastating bowler who could bowl fast and swing the ball late.

In fact, probably because the batsman had so little visual clues when facing him, they would find it hard to bat against him. There was no big leap at the wicket, no big front arm movement, no opportunity to work out exactly when the ball was coming over – and that made it extremely tough for a batsman. Ask anyone who faced Wasim Akram and they will say he was one of the most awkward to bat against, given that his bowling style wasn't classical.

Another bowler who didn't get off the floor very much or use hang time was Malcolm Marshall. But boy oh boy! Was he quick. Marshall had simply awesome speed generated from his body and hips, which created an enormous amount of arm speed.

Marshall was not very tall – he was quite a bit under six feet. Traditionally you think of a fast bowler as being a huge, athletic unit able to power the ball down at the batsman.

Marshall wasn't like that. He was a light, supple fast bowler with an open action. This meant nothing really stopped him in his action. There was relatively little front-foot impact for someone of his pace, and hardly any back-foot impact.

These factors contributed to his long career, which was amazingly injury free from much of the impact damage that fast bowlers tend to suffer. And whilst he did have a 'set' position (like Akram) that was momentary, just before he started his unwind in delivery, he didn't leap at the crease.

Both Akram's and Marshall's style of action didn't warrant hang time, and one could argue that a change would have disrupted their rhythm and speed. What would have been interesting is whether they would have benefited from using hang time as they were evolving as fast bowlers. The prospect that both of them may have been *even* faster is a startling thought. We shall never know. For this type of bowler they more than compensated for the lack of time spent in the air prior to delivery.

Darren Gough, by contrast, has *great* hang time and an action that's very easy on the eye. In 2005 we worked together to help improve his hang time by making some subtle changes to his bowling action. While the original changes were to help his straight lines and shoulder rotation, the overall effect altered his body position into a more upright posture during hang time. This in turn has taken some stress off his back and allowed his momentum to be further forward on driving through the crease (*see* figure opposite).

Note the forward rotation of hips and upper body control. His front-arm position is in the desirable 'L' shape so that he can rotate out of the crease when he drives this forwards and at the batsman. No movement here is above his eye line, meaning he is total control. He is centred, relaxed and ready to unleash his action in a sequential muscle stretch and con-

traction that comes from great understanding of his action.

Gough takes off from his left leg and stretches up the top half of his body into a 'set' position ready to bowl. It is during this point that he travels forward, at what appears to be a good metre or so in the air, in a controlled and technically superb holding position in preparation to impact his right foot at the crease. It's full of poise and balance and allows Gough to be extremely consistent. He is a very fast learner and one of the best fast bowlers I have ever had the privilege of working with. He's had a long and successful career at all forms of the game.

Brett Lee similarly gets up and into a 'hang time' position of strength and power just

Darren Gough with a perfect example of hang time.

prior to delivery. But Lee's set position has altered over the years due to stress fractures. He now gets front on and opens himself up so that his left-hand side can get out of the way, allowing his right-hand side to muscle through. And it all happens in straight lines. This not only looks imposing but is an important part of 'gathering' the action just prior to bowling. By climbing into this position everything appears to be held and 'tight'. There is nothing loose about the action – no flailing arms or wayward movements. It looks deliberate and it looks like a fast bowler should look.

In fact Lee's biomechanics are 99 percent perfect, which is why he can consistently bowl above 95mph and maintain high speed during long spells more often.

For me, there has only been one bowler who had it all – Allan Donald. It would have been very difficult to technically improve Donald's action, which I feel was flawless. And it started from his simply wonderful hang-time position. Other great fast bowlers, such as Kapil Dev, Imran Khan and Dennis Lillee, also perfected the art of hang time. If you can achieve it, it will help your performance too.

You can view this position between take off and landing as a checkpoint. You've already run in as far and fast as you need to. This jump to get airborne helps with a mental checkpoint to ensure you are lined up correctly and have all your body positions 'cocked'. In this intermediate part of your bowling action you should be ready to unfold your action when you make contact with the ground and then explode powerfully and smoothly through the crease. All the elements of your timing and control come from this. And the more you hold this position and relax, the easier you'll find it to obtain your rhythm.

You'll find that when bowlers shorten their hang time they tend to find it harder to get out of the crease and through their action. Their action starts to look a little flat; the timing appears wrong. It's as if they've lost their ability to bound in and create enough energy to travel through the air and so keep their momentum going. It's something that few coaches pick up on, which is why it goes unnoticed. Exceptions are bowlers with actions similar to Akram and Marshall, as mentioned earlier.

So what is an ideal hang time? And how high should you jump to achieve it? You are unlikely to get off the ground higher than a couple of feet, but this is perfectly adequate. In fact, if you are attempting to jump any higher pre-delivery I would suggest you are travelling in the wrong direction. That's because the purpose of hang time is not to get as high as possible, but to *travel* through the air. This is an important point. I have seen talented young bowlers with leaps to the wicket that are far too high. All they are achieving by this is to go up and down rather than forwards. Why waste energy travelling upwards? Everything should be going towards the batsman.

The mental thought process, therefore, is one of jumping towards the batsman, but in the air. Whilst in this motion you allow yourself to set up correctly with your front arm and ensure your upper body is relaxed but upright and not leaning back.

This is where your chest plays an important part. By taking a breath in as you jump, you'll help expand the chest cavity and give your upper body a strong stable position. It's as though you're being pulled up by your shirt as you jump.

How long you hang in the air will depend on how fast you're moving and what angle you jump up at. The ideal hang time will become obvious for your own action.

This is a 'try it and see' situation. If you run in too fast or jump too high, you may feel out of control at the crease, which will be the sign that it's not working. Everyone is different. Don't base your results on someone else. It will become clear what works for you. Experiment and exaggerate. Find out your own hang time and perfect it.

Front-Arm Load Up

A bowler's front arm is more than a rudder because it not only steers the rest of your body through its movement, but also dictates the shape of the bowling action.

Whether you choose to look over your arm or inside your arm is not important. That's a purely personal choice. What is important, however, is that your 'front-arm load up' doesn't throw you too far off balance.

I see many bowlers lifting their front arm way above their head, or throwing their front arm way across their body. The benefits of doing this are non-existent. In fact, the front arm ought to be a controlled movement that sets your body in balance so you can get forward in your action. So what would be an ideal position?

The ideal front-arm load up is hand at eye level or just above, giving you a visual cue. The arm would be in an 'L' shape at this point so that the hand can rotate outwards at the elbow towards the batsman. In other words, it helps line up the delivery, plus it maintains a momentum straight down at the target.

Refer again to the figure on page 30 showing Darren Gough. It's a perfect illustration of how to create a strong, non-bowling side. This is vital to act as a brake to pull against. You'll notice Gough is balanced and very relaxed in this position, but he's also 'set' and ready to bowl. It's something he does very well. It allows him 'time' to bowl and means he can stretch and contract all his main muscles for bowling in the right sequence.

This was the major change he and I made to his bowling in 2005. Previously, he threw his front arm across his body at right angles to the direction he was moving in. This slowed him down not only in the crease but also in his ability to 'get out' of the crease. The new position he has adopted is both stable and controllable. In other words, there's far less that could go wrong.

So the L-shape in a solid position is a key set up. This does two other things:

1. It maintains a level shoulder position so that your movement is controlled.

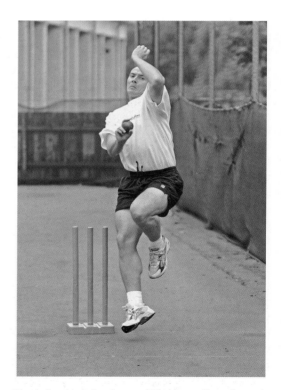

Just before back-foot impact. The front elbow shows the way to the batsman's stumps. The shape of the front arm helps keep the body driving at the target and maintains the balance of the movement without throwing the weight 'into reverse'.

2. It helps stretch the top half of the body out before you begin the drive and contraction of the bowling side.

When you begin the drive with your front arm at the batsman, you set the line for the rest of the body to follow.

Bowling-Arm Load Up

Hold your bowling hand in front of your eyes for a moment. Now check the bowling shoulder position. Keep looking at your bowling shoulder as you put your bowling hand behind

Taking the action back to just after take-off and still in hang time. Note the excellent front arm and bowling hand positions. This is a genuine power point for a bowler to be in.

your head. What do you notice?

You should see how your position changes quite dramatically. And you should notice the elbow position changing too.

Like the front-arm load up, the bowling-arm load up gives you a visual cue. So if you want to 'feel' controlled and disciplined, you'll probably need to see something in your peripheral eye line – either the front-arm or bowling-arm load up in other words. If you cannot see either, you have a problem.

There are bowlers who do not have a visual cue from either their front arm or bowling arm on load up. Effectively, both arms then do not rotate in the same plane, or the same circles, towards the batsman. This is known as 'shearing', which means a loss of consistency. You can probably think of international bowlers who suffer from this, which means that on good days they're great, but on bad days they're awful.

So bowling-arm load up in peripheral vision is a big visual cue for most bowlers. Controlling this movement so that the hand is at the side of the eye or just below it will assist in ensuring a smooth arm rotation in a straight line.

Hip Drive in a Sideways Game – Getting Some Snap in Your Bowling

I have read many books on bowling that talk about staying sideways towards the batsman *throughout* the bowling action. This is probably one of the most used, and confused, coaching theories that most bowlers have heard. And it's fundamentally flawed.

During a week at England's World Cup training camp in Port Elizabeth, I had to fly back to Cape Town and was browsing the books on offer in duty free. One was a cricket-coaching book, published in 2002, by a highly respected and leading coach with Western Province. I opened the book with much interest, eager to glean what gems he had to offer. I always love reading other coaches' ideas and will often adapt anything good from their observations and coaching methods. After all, we never stop learning. If there's anything great out there, I think it's worthwhile taking it on board.

Another view of front-arm positioning and bowling hand. Everything is happening in front of the bowler (not behind or above his head). Also note how the elbow again leads the action and is accompanied by the right knee. In fact, the right knee and right elbow should always stay together through the action, whether you have an open or sideways action. This ensures your hips and shoulders are always in line, thus helping to avoid 'counter-rotation' of hips and shoulders, and avoiding back injury.

Amazingly, I came to a section of the book where the author noted, after telling all bowlers to stay sideways on through the action, that some bowlers are actually chest on at delivery. It stopped me in my tracks. This was a revelation I didn't think I'd ever read in a traditional or conventional coaching book.

Let me tell you something to dispel any rumours, myths or legends about being sideways on. Every bowler is chest-on at the point of delivery. You cannot bowl straight unless you *are* chest on at delivery.

To gain power, to explode into an action and to maximise your strength – or in fact do just about anything that requires an increase in velocity – your hips provide the crucial clue. This is because the bulk of your power is likely to go where both your hips point.

Imagine a professional golfer, sideways on to the golf ball, taking away the club face above his head and then accelerating that club head towards the ball. What part of him moves to drive that ball? If he's right-handed, then it's his right hip. It drives towards the ball, accelerating his arms in the process, left hip rotating out of the way. At the point of contact the arms catch up, resulting in a turn of the upper torso, and the ball flies down the fairway.

A batter in baseball does exactly the same. A javelin thrower releasing a 90m (98yd) throw, a long jumper looking for height and distance on take-off, a tennis player serving, a martial arts expert kicking, a boxer throwing a punch – there are numerous examples of how this movement helps to maximise power. All of these require the hips to be driven through, creating a muscle stretch and contraction of the back and other key muscle groups. The truth is that at the point of impact, delivery or release, the powerhouse of the human body (hips) must face the way of the action itself *if you want maximum power*. The humble stone, when dropped into a pond, has power created at the centre, which then moves out towards the edge.

The feeling you need to imagine is driving your bowling hip into your front knee. In other words, it's as though the front leg tenses and locks, and the bowling hip is drawn towards it like a magnet. And it is definitely a *feeling*. Try it yourself now. (You'll find it's extremely hard to isolate this movement in the middle of bowling a ball.) That's why getting you to visualise and demonstrate the movement will help. If you are a right-arm bowler, your right hip is driven into your left knee through the crease. This gets you in position to deliver the ball with speed and accuracy at the target.

You're also going to be forcing your bowling knee through this position, too. It will initially seem as though your bowling knee is more important than your hip because it's easier to use it to drive the hip. But it isn't the sensation you want. In fact it's vital that you get the sense of your hip *leading* the action. By driving the hip, you switch on the muscle groups in your midriff section and back that will help increase speed. If you

At delivery. Hips and nose point at the batsman. Note the good power chest position. The feet are lined up straight to keep momentum going and take stress off the back. The front foot lands within the width of the hips, which is a natural position. This delivery allows for everything to continue down the pitch in a line.

This is a strength position prior to the delivery position shown earlier. It shows the front-foot impact and pull of the leg to help drive the right hip into the action. It acts as a braking force for the bowling side to power through. Note the right hip beginning its drive initially towards the front knee. The bowler's arm is still set well back, helping to stretch the muscle groups like a bow and arrow.

Just after delivery. The right hip and knee have been driven through naturally with energy by using the midriff section. The chest is also forward and muscling the action along the line of the ball. The front leg is offering full support as the front-foot flexion starts to begin the bowler's exit stride. Note the excellent seam position on the ball. This is a sign of great release position from the hand.

Halfway through the exit stride with the right hip, knee and shoulder all rotating to pull the body through 180 degrees and along the line of the ball. The head is straight and leads the action. The non-bowling arm is pulled through and out of the way.

simply use your bowling knee to do this it hasn't got quite the same effect.

Your hip leads your action for a split second. Your hips will be facing the batsman front on with your nose pointing at the target. It's as if you are 'whipping' your body from the middle outwards. You can recreate this visually by using your hand. Hold your arm and make a fist (at head level) pointing towards the ceiling as if you are going to punch it. Your elbow represents your feet, the wrist becomes your hips and the knuckles the top half of the body. Now rock your

knuckles backwards and push your wrist forwards to replicate the middle of the body being thrust forward. When you then rock your knuckles forwards, you'll see how the action might look.

It's just a simple way of helping you grasp the movement of the body through the crease. You should also feel this adding momentum when you 'cock' then 'uncock' the wrist in this way. There's a real 'snap' to the movement, which is often described by a bowler as exactly that when they are bowling well. You'll hear the comment of 'there was real snap in my action'. This hip drive and movement is what makes that feeling come alive. As the hips are in the centre of your body they have an amazing ability to create the fluidity of action that can appear effortless.

The great West Indian fast bowlers all seemed able to utilise this exceptional hip drive in their action. Most recently, Curtly Ambrose and Courtney Walsh had uncomplicated and easy actions, which served them well for many years. Both were tall men, but incredibly athletic. Ambrose switched his hips on at the key time to help generate pace from seemingly nowhere. Walsh used his hip to help rotate his entire body and bowling side through and out of his action.

It's not surprising that the hips are the power generators. Humans walk, and run, chest and hips on. It's probably the most natural position we adopt for adding momentum – for adding power. And our hips drive it. Our hips move the core of the body towards the way we wish to go.

Do you still think cricket is a sideways game? Just try and bowl, or bat or throw *literally* sideways on. It's impossible, or at least highly ineffective. That's because the body rotates in the middle to allow the powerhouse (hips) to add velocity to the action.

Chest Drive and the Ski Jumper

Of the many bowlers I have seen, there is one visual cue that sets a genuine quickie apart from a medium-pacer. Just watch them sideways on at the crease and see how far forward their chest drive is when they bowl.

If you were to draw an imaginary line, you'd generally find the faster the bowler, the further *driven* through the action they are with their chest. They are of course exceptions. But we're here to give you the perfect solution or best practice. And the really quick boys achieve an excellent chest drive.

The further forward they are – in other words driving the chest forward and down – the faster they bowl. This is what helps create the arc shape at delivery with the arm.

If you've ever watched ski jumping, you'll know what I mean. At take-off point, these amazing athletes are not far off parallel to the ground as they spring their weight towards their goal. It is an extreme example of how to use the body's natural movement to increase distance, but hopefully it will help you to exaggerate a main key point in

The chest drive captured in mid action. The bowling arm is still up and behind the bowler at this point, further enhancing the chest stretch. The harder and fuller the chest drive, the more power will be added to the arm pull and ball. Put simply, the further in front of the ball you can get with your chest, the better.

your mind. It would be impossible for the same ski jumper to gain any distance by being bolt upright.

For a fast bowler, the chest drive helps set up the unleashing of extra pace. When the chest is fully driven forward, it assists in the long bowling arm that is so desirable to create a slingshot effect. And whilst the arm is fluid and relaxed, the chest forms a solid position to work around. The results of this continue right through the crease as the bowler drives himself into the pitch.

This is an absolutely vital point. Throughout your bowling action the secret is to keep

The arm comes over in a straight line with the front foot and releases the ball directly above the shoulder. This is driven by the chest, which is the furthest forward along with the head.

relaxed. With the chest drive you'll want to *tense* your supporting chest wall muscles for maximum support. The sensation is that of fully inflating your chest, or breathing in and sticking your chest up and out. If you try this while sitting, you'll see exactly what I mean. As you're doing this, relax your shoulders and ease them back further behind you. Can you feel how this *adds* to the stretch of the chest and its position?

You've just isolated one of the *major* keys for fast bowling. If you want further proof (and you can do this while sitting), extend your bowling arm behind you so it points in the opposite direction to the way you face. *Now* inflate and extend your chest. Feel the stretch? Think about where you feel it. Under your arm maybe? In the chest itself? How about across the back of the shoulder? This one simple technique *switches* on the muscles you'll need to bowl faster.

Bear in mind you're feeling this extra and amazing stretch without trying to bowl. You're sitting down *without* a ball. Imagine how important that stretch becomes with a ball in your hand, running in at full speed, whilst driving through the crease at the batsman. With all the movements, momentum and other stretches adding to the drive, you can begin to see how vital this point is.

When you're actually bowling, the sensation is of being pushed in your back from behind whilst travelling through the crease. That's the amount of drive I am talking about. But it also needs to be controlled too. You can't just fling yourself headlong at the batsman – not just yet anyway.

When you try to bowl with a ball and drive your chest, you should find that the delivery is very full, or at least fuller than normal. You would expect this, as you are further forward in your action. So try it with a ball and see for yourself. If this is the case, it gives a clue as to how you can help bowl a better 'Yorker' (*see* Chapter 10).

Just before the front foot impacts, your bowling arm should be at full stretch behind you. This is part of hanging on the ball for as long as you can. The hips are already working to bring the body into line. But it is the 'long' bowling arm that will give you the 'catapult' feel to your action.

One other crucial fact about chest drive is that it will help keep your head going through straight. Since your head is one of the heaviest parts of your body, you will tend to follow through where the head goes. And bearing in mind we aim to keep everything going along one line, your chest drive is a factor in ensuring this happens.

I like to use other sports as analagies to reinforce a point. But there are so many in this case that I'm sure you can discover your own, whether it be from swimming, boxing, tennis or football.

Delaying the Bowling Arm

For a fast bowler, everything in the bowling action up to the point of delivery is primarily designed to accelerate the bowling arm. There is no mystery here once you understand

On front-foot impact the bowling arm is still at full stretch. The chest is starting its movement along with the right hip. This means your upper body is getting in front of the ball and beginning to angle towards the batsman.

Your bowling hand ought to be the furthest point behind you, slightly above and behind your bowling shoulder. This is because that position fully stretches major muscles groups. And it is these muscles that will ultimately speed up your bowling arm. By putting yourself in this position you have created 'torque' and stretch, as you would in an elastic band or a massive catapult. It's a 'bow-and-arrow' concept, with your body becoming the bow and the ball becoming the arrow – viewed from sideways on.

what's happening with your body. *The faster the arm comes over, the faster the ball comes out.* The secret is in knowing what you can do to increase the speed of that bowling arm, or give yourself a 'fast arm', as you hear some commentators say. But it seems strange then to say 'delay your bowling arm' if you are trying to make it as fast as possible.

Why is it therefore important to *hang* on the cricket ball as long as possible? That's a good question, and the answer is just as revealing. When you delay letting go of the ball it allows your muscles to stretch in sequence (hopefully) ahead of the actual ball release. This means the very last thing to come out of your delivery action is the ball. It is the delaying action of holding on to the ball that creates the power to deliver it in the first place.

Because a cricket ball weighs just 156gm (5½oz) it offers little resistance. Therefore it can be difficult to 'feel' the correct stretch required, and it is an odd position to try and replicate in slow motion. However, there is a quick and secret way of doing it.

In the privacy of your own home, simply hook your bowling hand underneath the top of a door frame and walk forward slowly until your hand is back and behind your shoulder. Next, point your hips straight ahead and lean carefully with your chest towards an imaginary batsman. If you are right-handed, drive the right hip ahead whilst bringing your left hip back. (Vice-versa for left-handers.) You should be able to feel the muscles stretching. By doing this you can also help your 'muscle memory'. This is the body's ability to recall a sequence of events subconsciously. By putting yourself in this important stretch position, you will be able to recall the feeling and thereby affect your skill in achieving this position.

If you have access to a gym or pulley system, you can also 'train' for this movement by using weights. Later on in this book there is a section on training, but using either a weighted ball, or some form of resistance,

will assist you in understanding the feeling.

In the bowling action itself, the further forward your body is the more of a 'boomerang' shape you'll be able to achieve via stretching your muscles. This position is going to be the maximum 'square-on' position you will get to in your action and your hips will be at their most extended point.

Think of yourself as a catapult or a fully pulled back bow about to fire off an arrow and you'll get the idea.

It is an exhilarating feeling being at

Viewed from sideways. You can see the chest is driven powerfully forward as the ball starts the journey up and over the shoulder. If you were to draw a line from the ball, along the edge of the body and to the back heel, you'd see the boomerang shape of the body. This is desirable for maximising speed. The deeper the curve, the better the position. This example is very good.

maximum stretch in this position. You feel as if everything is fully loaded and ready to go. You can sense the muscle stretch and the power posture in combination. There's a tremendous sensation of strength and poise, and the knowledge that you are about to unleash a thunderbolt of a delivery. Of all the key points in the bowling action, if you can master this one you'll be well on your way.

Long Levers, Maximum Rotation – Short Levers, Stunted Rotation

I recall a comment Ian Woosnam made when talking about driving the golf ball a long way.

He said 'A good big'un will always out hit a good littl'un'. His point was that if someone has longer arms and legs, they would create more power with an identical swing than someone who hasn't. If you think about it, it's undeniably true.

I think that many of us will also recall our physics days too, when diagrams were drawn to show how an object is accelerated faster when the same force is applied from a central point that has a longer arm instead of a shorter one. So the message here is twofold – keep your arms long and fully stretched so that you create more whip as well as utilise the muscle stretch correctly.

However, there is a development in coach-

Using a net backdrop to isolate the movement. Here in a relaxed position, the hand is hooked under the net whilst facing the way you want to bowl.

By pushing the bowling hip in the direction you want to bowl, you'll feel the power applied to your bowling hand hooked under the net. Nothing else moves except the hip. By experimenting with slightly different chest angles too, you'll feel additional power in your bowling arm.

ing to teach short levers. But this is a mistake. If by short levers, the message is meant to be *quick* levers, then the language simply needs to be changed. But *long, quick levers* are the very best combination.

To demonstrate a short lever, think of a propeller just 7cm (3in) across. It spins very, very quickly. Now make the propeller 3m (10ft) across. I think you'll find that's called a single-engine Cessna. If your levers are short, then your power is stunted.

One other consideration on short levers is that bowlers tend to collapse their non-bowling side, as it's usually the non-bowling arm that gets shortened. This ends up with

an elbow tucked tightly into the ribs and not doing very much.

You'll see many bowlers 'crunching' their elbows into their ribs (much more on this later). The arm can get blocked even though the idea is to get the opposite effect. We want to e–x–t–e–n–d the arm and then pull it down and hard so it helps drive the chest towards the batsman.

This is something the great Shoaib Akhtar does when he's really flying in. His arm is extended out towards the batter and then pulls quickly back to add acceleration to his trunk. He describes the feeling of 'grabbing the batsman's collar and yanking

Using the front arm as a long lever. Note the left knee moving along the same line as the arm. This helps to open up the hips. The front arm goes outwards in a forward movement and straight, not up and down. The hand drives towards the batsman to open the shoulders.

The front arm leads the action and will assist with the pull and shoulder rotation. Don't be tempted to shorten the arm here by pulling in your elbow. Instead, rotate around a strong head position and use your chest to continue driving your weight down the pitch.

it towards me', which I think perfectly sums up this movement.

Aussie Jeff Thomson and the awesome Alan Donald of South Africa also did this in their way. They made the most of their front arm levers. And it's no surprise that, with Shoaib, they are three of the greatest and fastest bowlers of all time.

In principle then, the acceleration of the body and the arms can create additional velocity to the ball. So the non-bowling arm becomes important here since it is the start of the power. I will always remain a fan of driving the arm outwards towards the batsman and downwards to help push the chest forward and further rotate the shoulders, which is a vital movement.

Imagine the shoulders for a moment. The non-bowling shoulder leads the action, and the bowling shoulder finishes it off. In other words, the shoulders swap places by rotating towards the batsman as a swimmer does when doing the front crawl. If there were a faster way to swim, then by now someone would have done it. This is the secret to ensuring all your power is being transferred correctly from one side to the other.

Take a look at the truly quick bowlers of the past decade: Allan Donald, Brett Lee and Shoaib Akhtar being just three. Their shoulder rotations are immense – very full and completely finishing off the bowling actions. All three also happen to follow about 99 percent of this book

The arm in mid action being used to pull out and towards the batsman. The bowling side is coiled and ready to take over.

Note the non-bowling arm is out and away behind the bowler and not 'tucked in' where it can block power and cause an obstruction. Also, because the shoulders are joined, the pulling away of the non-bowling arm helps accelerate the bowling arm. This all happens in straight lines as usual.

correctly in the first place so it is little surprise that they have, at varying times, occupied the number one slot for being the world's fastest bowler. All have a huge sweep of the bowling arm plus sensational chest drives and good hip actions too.

So is the perfect action a result of some natural birthright? No, but a high degree of natural ability is required to be truly fast. The rest can be taught and, quite often, good fast bowlers can be created out of ordinary ones. This book is about *optimising* what you already have, not getting you to start again. It's an exciting thought to know that you can be awash with extra pace and accuracy by making simple, proven alterations.

The full shoulder rotation showing weight transference, but along a straight line. This is known as 'finishing off' the action. The chest and hips are through and the head is still and balanced.

What to do With Your Non-Bowling Arm

Because the shoulders are attached, what you do with your non-bowling arm affects the arm delivering the ball. If you pull your shoulder behind you the other one comes forward. Try it now while sitting. Pull your non-bowling shoulder behind you and look at the other shoulder. And this is what happens without you trying to bowl.

So it doesn't pay to get 'lazy' with it (although instead of using 'lazy', I prefer the description 'easy'). The majority of bowlers are not able to make the most of their action without the non-bowling arm driving forcefully.

Generally, it pays to 'throw' the arm towards the batsman – helping to maintain a drive down the pitch. Think of this movement as like a karate chop. But (and this is where it starts to go wrong for many) the arm should then rotate down and back in a semi-circle, rotating the shoulders through 180 degrees.

Halfway through your action. This shows how important the extended bowling arm is. Note the chest and hips and slight forward angle of the trunk. You can almost see the power being applied to the bowling shoulder and arm.

Unless this happens, the bowling shoulder cannot replace the non-bowling one (as viewed by the batsman). The quicker you can do this, the quicker you will deliver the ball.

Unfortunately, there is a trend among some coaches to advise the bowler to drive the non-bowling elbow downwards at delivery. However, this can 'crunch' the body into itself and make it easier to collapse the action. Worse still, it tends to throw the bowler towards gulley with the top half of the body, unless he is very careful. This is because a bowler can 'fall off' his action. It's a problem I've seen recently with some County and International bowlers. Having spoken to a few during specialist nets, they have admitted it was advice

The bowling shoulder replaces the non-bowling shoulder and you can see the back of the bowler as he exits his action. This is called 'finishing off' the action and is what you need to aim for.

given to them at top-level coaching sessions.

My fear for bowlers, who drive their non-bowling arm down during delivery, is that they will stop their momentum and block off the movement, causing energy to be lost. The aim ought to be to get this non-bowling arm back and away behind you, pointing fingers skyward as a natural part of a full rotation to help drive the bowling shoulder at the batsman.

Lining Up Your Feet

It is extremely hard to bowl with any great pace or consistency if your feet work against each other. By that I mean that, if you're trying to bowl straight down the pitch, make sure the foot you bowl off doesn't land closer to the leg side than your back foot. This will 'close off' your action and make it very unlikely that your hips can point at the target.

There are always bowlers who have this set-up with their feet and yet still get to the top. Dean Headley and Matthew Hoggard of England both have these issues, and both have remarkably similar actions. Technically, it has affected their ability to bowl truly fast and I feel that Matthew Hoggard, in particular, is probably 5–8mph slower than he ought to be, which could have put him at 90mph. Both bowlers have learned to compensate with a fast 'twist' of the upper trunk, but also tend to topple off their actions due to this.

Another group of bowlers who do this are left-armers. Almost exclusively, the vast majority of left-arm bowlers close off their hips by landing their front foot across their back foot. I can only imagine it's because they have a misguided idea that this will help the ball swing. But, as we know, swing comes from ball and wrist position.

Whatever the reason, it will mean that the vast majority lose speed. That's why the great fast bowlers are rarely left-armers. Throughout history you can count on a few fingers those truly quick left-arm bowlers. By setting up in the wrong position, it's very hard to maximise speed.

So, if you are able to get your base right at the crease with your feet, you are in a position to make the rest of your action line up correctly. If you stand facing the way you want to bowl and look down at your feet, this would be an ideal line up for the feet line up at delivery. Rotate your bowling arm. Now face the same way and line your feet as if walking a tightrope and just slowly rotate your bowling arm. Can you feel how it restricts your ability to bowl?

Here's how to get it right: Draw a line in the turf from the front crease to the back crease, straight down the pitch. Stand either side of this line with feet a hip's width apart so that the line cuts your body in half. You now have the ideal width apart, from back-foot impact to front-foot impact when you bowl.

By keeping that line down the centre of your body, and your feet either side of it through your action, you ensure your hips are 'switched on'. This is a power position that your body can naturally work to.

Showing a 'closed' front foot position relative to the back foot. A bowler with this type of feet line up will have to bowl 'round' their front foot and lose pace. The bowling arm can also tend to get pushed out and a slight 'round arm' looking action develops. From this position, a bowler is likely to bowl outswing because of dragging the ball from leg to off in their action.

Showing the biomechanically correct front-foot line up where the front foot lines up with the right hip and the left foot with the left hip. This turns the power on and allows the hips through whilst using the core muscle groups (midriff area). The result is that the body moves in a straight line and maximises both speed and accuracy by having a stable base.

It also means you have no twisting of the trunk on impact. This is one of the main reasons stress fractures and soft tissue damage occurs. So if there's no twisting of the spine – just a simple forward motion of the hips and chest – you will feel 'free' at the crease. Also, there's nothing to stop you following through straight.

Bowling should feel natural and work with the way the body wants to move. Why make it hard for yourself?

Bowling Off the Front Foot

One of the simplest ways to check if a bowler is driving through the crease correctly is to see when they start to deliver the ball. Frankly, without planting your front foot correctly, you will not be making the most of your body when delivering the ball.

There are many bowlers who effectively deliver the ball with their weight not correctly transferred from back leg to front foot. The motion of delivering the ball *must* take place

Showing an exaggerated 'open' front-foot position. A bowler with this type of feet line up can have problems controlling their line since their weight is going towards gulley. Bowlers like this tend to 'spear' the ball in at a batsman or bowl inswing. However, because the hips are open, a lack of pace is not usually one of the problems (unless the body motion keeps the bowler going off the pitch). This makes it harder to move the ball towards slips, which is a dangerous delivery for a batsman.

Bowling off the front foot. This is a position that's all about timing. Everything before the action comes into line over the front foot. The weight is transferred from back to front foot. The point of release is fractionally inside the front foot and over the bowling shoulder.

47

off the front foot. If this seems obvious, why is it that far too many coaches don't spot it?

The front foot acts as a braking force for you to pull against. It is also your solid position that will help add integrity to your action. Without this solid base, you have to make up for it in other areas, and I'd rather you get it right from the start.

The front foot is the point from which you launch. Whether it is with a cricket ball, baseball or javelin, you deliver off the front foot from a solid, firm base.

A quick note here about back-foot impact. As mentioned earlier, to get maximum power and pace through the crease you will need to

Showing the front foot and leg bracing to allow delivery of the ball. The weight has gone from back leg to front as the ball is coming over. But the ball isn't delivered until a firm base is established and the upper body can drive ahead.

drive the hips through. This can only take place when you push off the back foot. So the back foot begins the drive of the action. It helps the motion of the core – the midriff area – to transfer to the front foot for delivery. It is this exchange of movement from back foot to front that creates the pace as far as the core of the body is concerned.

We've all seen the big lads who, in theory, should be really fast bowlers. They are blessed with a large physique. They appear very strong. They are tall. They look, off their long run-ups, as if the ball is going to rocket out of their hand when they let it go. But, instead, the ball is delivered like a handful of confetti. You feel that if they carried on running, they may even beat the ball to the other end. There's nothing 'behind' the ball – it has no 'weight' to it.

In this situation, I have often found that the main culprit is non-transference of weight from the back leg to front foot correctly. Yet when you watch these people bowl, it is hard to identify the problem. That's why progress goes unchecked and the bowler rarely ever gets it right. Instead, they rely on 'doing something' with the ball to compensate. Imagine being able to bowl 2–3m (about 2–3yd) quicker *and* 'do something' with the ball.

Bowlers need to ensure that if they rock back at delivery (which was very fashionable to coach in previous years) they get their weight onto the front foot before they bowl. Otherwise, we'll have a nation of medium-pacers and trundlers.

Exit Stride

The exit stride is the first stride you take out of your action, and in a way it's a key factor to ensuring everything you've done is correct.

So it's vital you manage to exit your action with your head and chest leading.

Again, Darren Gough is a great exponent of this. We have worked to change his front arm position so that he is now able to use it for leverage. This enables him to exit his bowling action with head and chest leading. By doing this well, you'll find in your own action you have wonderful balance. It also means you can keep moving in a straight line, directly at the batsman.

Brett Lee is a very visible example of how to exit the crease with venom, as are Allan Donald, Shoaib Akhtar and Shane Bond. All are great exponents of using their momentum in straight lines to take them out of the crease.

Some bowlers veer away from the batsman on follow through, for example South African Makaya Ntini. He slightly loses pace and will also lose some consistency at times because he has to compensate with his bowling arm to correct the non-straight-line rotation out of the crease. His exit stride goes away from a straight line. Yet he is a great bowler in spite of this, because he does so many other things right.

If you can maintain a strong exit stride you'll keep everything on track for longer and have more control of accuracy and speed. Again, look at the fastest bowlers in the world. Watch their actions. You'll note that

The first stride out of the action is the exit stride. It tells a great deal about a bowler. All movement should continue along the line of the ball. If it doesn't, it usually means there's a problem in the action somewhere.

Halfway through the exit stride. Note the exceptional hip and knee drive. Also, there's excellent shoulder rotation and good non-bowling arm take away. The head is balanced too. Aim for this in your own bowling.

The top half of the body after the exit stride keeps the weight moving towards the batsman.

the majority consistently have a strong exit stride. It's no coincidence.

Follow Up on the Ball

I know it sounds obvious but following the ball down the pitch after you let it go is important. Yet some bowlers do not follow through correctly. With momentum behind you, you need a runway – just like a plane landing. It doesn't just stop the instant it hits the tarmac and neither should you.

Here's a rule of thumb. Follow through down the pitch about half the length of your run-up. If you run in 20m (22yd), finish halfway down the pitch. If you run in 40m (44yd), you ought to be shaking hands with the batsman. There

are two reasons why. The first is it *looks* right. Remember, you are meant to be a fast bowler, so mean it. Second, when your weight transference is correct at the crease, you *cannot fail* to follow through properly.

If you think you've got it right and you are not following through half your run-up, you might just be running in too far.

When you have delivered the ball, rotated your shoulders and driven your chest and hip through your action, chances are your immediate follow through step will be dramatic. And it needs to be because the momentum will force you forward.

Your follow through should also be as straight as possible. It will show if you have veered off towards the offside and is a sign your momentum isn't at the batsman.

CHAPTER 5

Accuracy

We have now covered how to approach practice for biomechanics. Now let's look at practising specific skills. Here I will get all misty eyed and traditional on you. (Yes, I am a traditionalist in certain areas.)

I firmly believe that 'target' practice is the only conscious way to learn how to bowl accurately – whether it is for line or length. Irrespective of your style of action, it is only by being consistent that you can become a quality bowler.

A golfer basically plays target golf all the way round a golf course. Tiger Woods can do amazing things with a golf ball but, above all else, he knows how to land it in the exact area needed for each shot he's playing, and about to play. A darts player will practise for hours at hitting a certain part of the board – doubles, trebles, the bullseye and so on – because he knows that unless he is precise he cannot compete. A snooker player knows how to make contact with the cue ball, not only to pot the ball but also to leave a position for the cue ball on the next shot. Sport is driven by the ability to be exact. Cricket, and in particular fast bowling, is the same.

The great success of world-class bowlers is that they are usually so accurate. They will bowl a series of deliveries in very much the same place time after time. This grouping is known as 'clusters' and it's something to strive for in your own game.

Bowling clusters requires you to keep dropping the ball around the same spot as often as you can. You may have seen TV coverage where they show you how many deliveries from a bowler are landing on which part of

the pitch. You'll see from this that the more concentrated the clusters on the right length, the better the bowler.

Now you can duplicate this in your own practice by target bowling.

When I was growing up, my target bowling was achieved by aiming at a couple of tin cans placed at a good length. It didn't even have to be in a net, because the pitch quality didn't matter. Often, I would go to the local park or cricket outfield. I'd put a sweater down as the stumps at the bowler's end, mark out a crease with my boots and put the cans about 14m (16yd) away on an imaginary line with off stump. It would have been easier to mark 5–6 paces from the batsman's set of stumps – it is the same thing – but there was something about striding out the distance and getting to 'know' just how far it was from the crease at my end.

The other great thing is that you can practise this on almost any surface you want. It doesn't have to be in the nets. It can be in a field, on a beach, in the school playground, artificial surface, or a back yard. It might involve being a bit creative but that's part of the fun.

This type of accuracy training is not new. It takes place through many of the original cricket coaching award schemes. As a child I recall bowling at a target whilst trying to hit the stumps at the same time, and getting points for both. This was like a 'proficiency award' system.

Some of my friends used this to develop games we played long into the summer evenings. We bowled for hours before our parents came to the playing field and called us in. Many of those accuracy games carried on over days and weeks. What we didn't realise at the time was that we were grooming our ability – we simply found it a fun thing to play. What's more, it became a test of accuracy that is easy to see. Immediately the results are obvious.

For your own practice, the size of the target to aim at is entirely your choice. You might choose an oblong sheet measuring 45 × 91cm (18 × 36in) for example. This helps you look along the line you are bowling when it's placed covering middle and off stump to outside off stump. It acts as a corridor to focus in on.

If you want something *really* challenging you could use an old CD, which is about two ball widths wide and deep. When you can hit this consistently, you'll be on your way to international cricket. But the ultimate – the best of the best – is achieved by simply placing a cricket ball on the exact spot you want to hit. This practice is called 'cricket snooker'. You place a series of balls on parts of the pitch and attempt to hit them in sequence. This shows maximum control over your bowling and it's great fun to try. If you can hit it one out of

twenty times you're doing well. That's how tough it ought to be. If you hit it regularly you have the ability to be an international bowler.

If all these things seem obvious, let me assure you that few bowlers actually practise them. Bowlers bowl at a stump. But they rarely use a target on the pitch to aim at too. And that's a great error because it helps programme the brain into understanding the timing of the ball release from the hand. When you train enough times this way it becomes automatic. Your mind and body will synchronise to help deliver the ball where you want it to go.

So you need to get back to basics with accuracy. You need to develop the nagging ability to be precise in your bowling. This is the one part of your game, above all others, where there is no short cut. You cannot cheat yourself here because you will be found out unless you can bowl with control.

The advanced biomechanics you are now familiar with will help you *duplicate* your action correctly. The actual physical part of landing the ball where you want it to go is down to how much you practise it.

CHAPTER 6

Seam Bowling –
Line and Length

In the early days I did strive for pace. I was a young tearaway fast bowler and tried to run in and bowl as fast as I could. I often bowled too short and early statistical results would show that when you take 1/90 and 2/120 you must be doing something wrong. After a while, when you look at those perform-ances, you ask, 'what do I have to do to get it right?' One had to look at fitness, at develop-ing an efficient technique. The mental side of it was very important. Having belief and confidence in oneself was important. Obvi-ously it was important to adapt to various pitch conditions and analyse the weak-nesses of various batsmen. I went through a number of paces. First from being a teara-way fast bowler to a more thoughtful bowler who was physically better and had a good technique. The final phase over the last ten years was operating off a shortened run up, operating off about fifteen paces. That made me clinically efficient. While I lacked a yard or so in pace, I made up for it with better control and the ability to bowl for longer periods of time. I could still bowl the odd quicker ball that would put the batsmen on their backsides. My results were three times more effective in the last ten years than what they were in the first eight or nine.

Richard Hadlee

It doesn't really matter at what pace you bowl, you simply *have* to do something with the ball. That's the obvious truth about bowling.

A good batsman will take full toll of you if you can't move the ball about. And a great batsman will have the mindset that you're simply there to put the ball into play.

This is especially true on easy paced pitches. Everything appears to be in favour of the batsman on decks like this. That's why you need to learn the art of seam bowling – even if you are a swing bowler.

I recall asking a bowler on one of the English County Academies what type of bowler he thought of himself as. He told me he was a swing bowler. So I asked him 'What happens if it doesn't swing?' It wasn't a trick question but he didn't have an answer. That's exactly why all quickies need to know how to seam the ball.

Seam bowlers and swing bowlers have slightly different thought processes. A seam bowler 'hits the pitch' hard, whereas a swing bowler tends to 'kiss the pitch' with the ball. It's a more skimming delivery when the ball swings, plus the damage is done by move-ment in the air rather than off the pitch. So the seaming delivery is designed to be bowled into the pitch a lot more. This affects the length you bowl too, because a seaming deliv-ery can be highly effective from a different length than a swinging delivery.

Where would you say is the right length for a bowler to be pitching the seaming ball? Driving length? A good length? Back of a length? It all depends on the pitch, the batsman and, of course, the bowler.

Some bowlers are very tall, such as Steve Harmison. He relies on this height to get extra bounce and discomfort the batsman. So his natural pitching length will be invariably shorter than, say, Malcolm Marshall's was. Harmison's ability to draw the batsman into playing a shot is the key. He is able to produce steepling bounce and is awkward to judge as the ball is being released from such a high relative release position due to his stature. This was also true of West Indian Curtly Ambrose and other great fast bowlers who are around 2m (6ft 6in) and above.

You have leeway on length dependent upon your pace, height and pace of the pitch. It is up to you to judge it for yourself, but here's a clue. Irrespective of anything else, you should be drawing the batsman in to playing a stroke they perhaps didn't want to. This also gives you a hint about the *line* you want to be aiming at.

The length will not be too full otherwise the batsman can hit the ball without having to adjust to any seam movement, and it won't be too short so that he has adjusted to it already. The bat is only about 10cm (4in) wide, which means that to find the edge you only have to move the ball half of that distance. So we're not talking about huge movements off the pitch.

It would make sense then to give the batsman as little time as possible to make that adjustment. You'll ideally be trying to bring the batter forward and pushing at the ball. And if you can induce him to go hard at the ball, chances are, if it's an edge, it will carry to slip or keeper (gulley or backward point if it's wider).

To sum all this up, my suggestion is to try to hit the splice of the bat as the batsman goes forward. Naturally, he's trying to make contact with the ball from the middle of his bat. And you're trying to avoid that.

As a seam bowler regularly hitting the seam, you will find that you're likely to get more bounce. When the ball hits the seam it can do very unusual things. For a start, the seam is raised relative to the rest of the ball. But it is most likely to get a kick from the pitch when it does this and bounce a bit higher than when it doesn't hit the seam.

If you are quick, you'll find it tempting to hit the splice of the bat with the batter going on the back foot. This is fine on hard pitches or where you are genuinely quick compared to the batsman.

Alex Tudor of England is someone who hits the bat very hard. As was Devon Malcolm. Both bowled a 'heavy ball' as it is

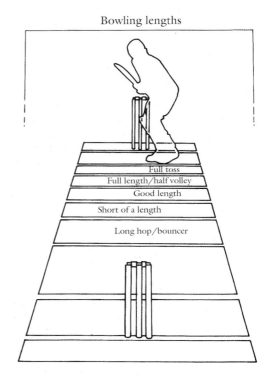

Bowling lengths

The various bowling lengths. The ideal pace to bowl most of the time is either a good length or just short of a length. The faster you are the more you're likely to bowl a fraction shorter and get away with it. A swing bowler is always looking to have a batsman driving from a good length or full length: a seam bowler from a good length to just short of a good length.

called. The tendency here is for those bowlers to be hitting the bat splice with the batsman back in his crease. But more success can be had when you draw the batsman in to front-foot shots.

Think about your own game for a moment. Are you looking to get a batsman on the front foot or back foot? As a quicker bowler like those mentioned, you'd be harder to play if the batsman was in two minds. You know he wants to play off the back foot, but really knows he *ought* to be forward due to the length.

This is where you can have a tremendous victory over the batter. He'll end up getting stuck in the crease. And you have the chance of an LBW, bowled or caught behind.

This brings us neatly on to line. How straight should you bowl? How wide should you bowl? And does it matter?

Yes, it does matter. You'll find the margin for error in both line and length decreasing as you go up the levels of cricket. Higher levels of batters play the straight ball away through the leg side. By that I mean they work it with a straight face (and sometimes not) into gaps through mid-on and mid-wicket, especially left-handers facing right-arm bowlers.

It's been a development of the modern game and has helped increase notional run rates of Test cricket up to around four and over and beyond.

That's why you'll hear commentators such as the legendary Geoff Boycott talk about the 'corridor of uncertainty'. It's that 5–15cm (2–5in) channel just around off stump and outside. To imagine this, think of the red line the TV replays put in to line up the wickets. Now move that line across so it touches the batsman's off stump. You're now highlighting the corridor. And when the ball is bowled in this, the batsman finds it hard to decide what to play at and what to leave.

The best recent example of this has been Andrew Flintoff going around the wicket to Adam Gilchrist. The left-handed Gilchrist, a wonderful batsman averaging more than fifty at Test cricket, really struggles against Flintoff when he goes around the wicket and targets just outside his off stump. The England team have worked out that Gilchrist cannot select which balls to leave alone regularly with this angle of attack. And due to Flintoff's ability to seam and swing the ball both ways, it has caused great issues for Gilchrist who has fallen to Flintoff almost one in two times.

So this 'corridor' is important. If you are seaming the ball in this slice of the pitch, you have a great chance to be a very fine bowler. Someone who exploits this to perfection is Australian Glenn McGrath. He is tall and disciplined, with a robotic action (and a good one biomechanically) and drops the ball time after time in the same area of the pitch. He has the ability to run the ball away off the wicket and back into the batsman too. And that's very tough to bat against when bowled so accurately on a good length.

Batsmen like to free their arms when they play. They like to get their hands through the ball and hit it cleanly. When you bowl a tight line to them with no width outside off stump and not too straight so they can't hit you away on the leg side, it's much harder to score runs.

This type of accuracy will build up pressure. A batsman feels happiest when he is scoring freely. But to dry up those runs and to stifle his game creates pressure. It means that even if the ball is not moving all over the place, he can make mistakes by getting bogged down. So bowling well is all about discipline.

You must learn discipline in your bowling and ally it with patience. Cricket is largely a waiting game. Sure, you can make things happen and you should always strive to. *But if you are disciplined and patient you will succeed more times than not.* You are in the business of enticing the batsman into making an error, particularly at higher levels where less mistakes are made by everyone. A build up of pressure goes a long way to creating a feeling that the batsman has to do *something* to break free.

Legendary bowlers, such as Kiwi Richard Hadlee and South Africa's Shaun Pollock, like to bowl maidens for fun. It's easy to see why. When you continually bowl 'dot' balls, you dry up the opposition's scoring rate. They get stuck and you take control. Some bowlers are just as happy to bowl large amounts of maidens as they are taking wickets. And sometimes a bowler sending down maiden after maiden *creates* wickets at the other end for someone else to take. That's why great bowlers hunt in pairs.

The secret is to be very focused on exactly where you want to be aiming the ball and then stick to it. Now let's look at the actual seam movement itself.

There are two types of seam delivery. One moves the ball away from the batsman and one moves it in to the batsman. Because a cricket ball is not a perfect sphere, there are a two ways of bowling them; both can be very effective.

The seam stitching is noticeably raised. If the ball is bowled so that the seam hits the pitch when it bounces, this irregularity can cause the ball to deviate sideways in its path This gives seam movement.

Corridor of uncertainty

Offside

Legside

Deliveries landing in the highlighted corridor cause the most difficulty for the batsman

The corridor of uncertainty. Bowl as many deliveries in your career in the corridor as you can. It starts from hitting the top of off stump and continues for roughly two ball widths to the off side.

A ball delivered just fractionally short of a good length and in the corridor leads to problems for the batsman. He does not know whether to go forward or back and whether to play it or leave it.

In order to achieve this effect, you'll usually need to deliver the ball with the seam held upright, with rotation about a horizontal axis (likely to be towards you as you pull down on the ball). This avoids the dreaded 'scrambled seam', which looks as if the ball is wobbling and means you haven't let the ball go correctly.

By keeping your wrist position 'locked' in place, you can ensure the release of the ball is upright. This keeps the seam aligned vertically as it travels towards the batsman, making it likely that the ball will bounce *with the seam* on the pitch.

The direction and degree of deviation from a straight path are dependent on the small-scale alignment of the seam and any irregularities in the pitch surface. The idea, put simply, is to make sure the seam impacts with the pitch first (rather than the leather part of the ball).

If the raised seam makes impact with the pitch on a good length at 80mph (128km/h), what's going to happen? Nobody knows. And that's exactly why a good bowler, who hits the seam every time, can be so devastating.

You know when you're hitting the seam regularly. The ball will come back to you with grass in the seam, which you'll need to pick

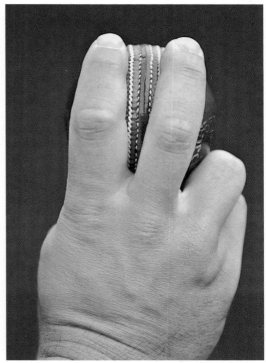

Batsman's view of the classic seam bowler's grip and wrist position. First and second fingers hold the ball firmly but not overly tight. Use the pads of the fingers. The thumb rests either on the seam underneath or by the side of the seam to keep the ball balanced. The 'ticklish' part of the wrist is kept facing the batsman. This helps keep the seam upright through the air.

View from behind the bowling hand of the classic seam bowler's grip. From this position, a simple flick of the wrist during delivery helps counter-rotation of the ball, thus making it more stable in flight.

out. It's perfectly OK to pick grass out of the seam. However, if you miss the seam, particularly on harder pitches, you'll see the leather of the ball come back scuffed where it impacted on the pitch.

If you're bowling on a batsman-friendly pitch, it's even more important to be hitting the seam regularly. It protects the ball and also means you are likely to create problems for the batsman.

Ensuring you hit the seam therefore gives you a massive advantage, not least because a sheer amount of deviation is caused by seam, which is chaotic and unpredictable. Sometimes the ball will do very little. At other times it will 'bite' in the pitch and jag quite noticeably in one direction or another. There's no way of telling and you can not accurately predict the amount a ball will move. If you can not predict this as the bowler, then neither can the batsman. He's now making guesses. He's assuming. And he's hoping he's right. When you have the batsman guessing, you're in control.

The second way of bowling a seamer is by holding the seam at an angle and rolling the fingers over the surface of the ball. This will produce a deliberate off cutter, where the ball veers away from the offside when it bounces on the pitch, or leg cutter, which veers away from a right-handed batsman.

Strictly speaking, this is imparting a little spin or rotation to the ball and encourages it to move in the direction you have rolled your fingers. You can employ 'cutters' of this sort to considerable effect. However, this type of delivery will be slightly slower than if you simply bowl with the seam upright, hoping for movement one way or the other.

Another benefit is that the seam may 'kick' if it impacts the pitch, further adding to the movement by enhancing the bounce of the ball. It may also come out slightly slower, since you'll be rolling your fingers over the ball rather than getting them behind the ball as you would do in the first example. But that's no bad thing. Remember it is your job to keep the batsman uncomfortable by mixing things up. If you get

By rolling the fingers over the top of the ball on release, you can get rotation on it. This is the finish position of an off cutter, which is aimed to cut back into a right-hand batsman from outside off stump. The index finger does much of the work pulling the ball from off to leg.

This is the finish of a leg cutter. The middle finger does much of the work, rolling the ball from leg to off. This delivery is aimed to cut away to slip from a right-hand batsman. Both the leg cutter and off cutter are suitable for damp or slow pitches.

too rigid and obvious, a good batsman can start to 'work you out'. It is a good idea to have other deliveries at your disposal.

In baseball terms, think of a pitcher. A pitcher will have half a dozen varieties of delivery by changing the grip and release of the ball from the hand. Even subtle changes can have dramatic effects. It's all done to fool the batsman, to get him to mistime the ball, hit it in the air or simply not make any contact with it at all. So there is much you can learn from this.

My suggestion is you perfect the seaming delivery. And then become very, very good at bowling what *looks like* the same delivery, but is in fact something else.

CHAPTER 7

Swing Bowling – Risk and Reward

Why is swing bowling 'risk and reward'? The answer is quite simple.

To swing the ball, you are pitching the ball further up to the batsman, inviting him to take a drive at it. This is where you start to take the *risk*, because you're tempting the batsman with a delivery that allows him to play an attacking shot. The majority of batsmen simply *love* to drive. So when they see the ball around a full length it's a bit like getting three cherries up on a slot machine. However, a batsman's strength is often his weakness.

This is where the *reward* kicks in. You *want* the batsman to take a drive at you and edge it for a catch or miss it and get bowled. He is fooled into thinking it's a delivery he can dispatch easily for a boundary, but you lure him into something he wishes he hadn't played at.

For added effect, you may have even taken fielders out of cover and put them in at slip. This creates a yawning gap that even the most conservative batsman cannot resist after a while. And although he *still* knows you're trying to do that, his instinct for the booming drive takes over.

Then, of course, there's the swing you can get before the batsman is aware of it. And there's nothing like it. It can happen to a new batsman, or with a new ball first up (although the current new balls swing less than they used to since they have a plastic lacquer rather than hand polishing).

As an opening bowler, you get a brand new shiny cherry in your hand. It's deep red and perfectly formed. You run your fingers either side of the white seam. The umpire calls 'play' and you start your run in to the wicket. The adrenalin pumps. When you let it go, the new ball gets down the other end and starts to swing. It swings very late and just enough. The batsman is beaten all ends up, stumps flattened, feet nowhere. Quite rightly, you'd probably point out where the pavillion is (match fee permitting), not that he would have forgotten how to get back there.

Swing bowling can be *really* dangerous for a batsman. Particularly when he has just come in. That's because there's a change of direction in the air, which starts to ring alarm bells as he lines himself up to play.

As his innings progresses and a batsman knows you are swinging the ball, he will attempt to change his game to play it. Or he will at least be affected by what you are trying to do with the ball. You'll find he starts to leave deliveries he doesn't want to and is playing at deliveries he really shouldn't have. And all because of that magical swing from your hand to his bat.

If you can get the angle right, so it appears to swing later (closer to the batsman), then it causes some serious issues for him. It really is all about risk and reward.

So you won't be surprised to know the condition of the ball plays a key role in helping the ball swing. It's vital that you work on the ball to keep it in good condition. This is not just the job of the bowler either. All the fielders have to help, as do other bowlers, including spinners. I am always amazed that fielders and spinners don't help with keeping a new ball in as great a condition as possible during an innings. You only get one new ball at the start of the innings and it's everyone's job to ensure it's shined up, clean and protected.

The ball is your *asset*. So here's a checklist to bear in mind:

- Keep the seam clean of mud, dirt or grass. It helps with seam movement if there is more to grip the pitch, rather than having the seam caked with rubbish.
- Keep *one* side of the ball shiny. For there to be swing on the ball as the lacquer wears off, one side of the ball must be polished (more on reverse swing later). Use spit, sweat and elbow grease to keep the ball as 'mirror like' as you can. You are trying to create a difference between the state of the two sides of the ball to get swing.
- Keep the ball dry. Nothing ruins swing in a cricket ball as much as damp.
- Appoint someone other than a bowler to be responsible for shining the ball and keeping it in good condition. Usually a player fielding in the inner ring who knows what is required. Make sure the ball is always passed tothem on its way back to the bowler.
- Make sure everyone in the team knows and understands about the ball condition, what's expected and how to maintain it.

I can't stress enough how a well-kept cricket ball can make an amazing difference in your ability to bowl sides out regularly. It's *your* ball, keep it in good condition.

Now all you have to do is *actually* swing the ball. And here's how.

The seam on a cricket ball acts, to a large extent, like the rudder on a ship. If you hold the ball with the seam upright and facing one way it will swing that way. If you point it facing the opposite way it swings the opposite way. Simple, but nonetheless they are the basics for swing bowling.

So when you get the angle of the seam right, you'll find the ball will take that route. Research by clever men with glasses shows that angle to be around 20 degrees from straight on. In other words, the swing will follow the seam. To assist in this, you need one side highly polished and the other side less so. Of course, if the ball is brand new, then both sides are highly polished. This is where it gets interesting.

The new ball can really swing given the correct wind conditions. Where the breeze is in the right direction, just point that seam and watch it hoop. This is how a new ball swings. It is the seam position and speed of bowler that affects the amount of swing. The optimum speed for swing bowling is around 72mph (115km/h). The faster you bowl over that, the less it swings – it still swings, but the amount of diversion from the straight becomes less and less until you get around the 90mph (144km/h) mark, when the ball then has a tendency to go into 'negative' swing, or what we refer to as reverse swing. Again, the condition of the ball affects this too. But a new ball can reverse swing due to airflow over the ball's surface. To deliver any swing you need a firm wrist position to keep the seam upright. The reason is that by producing counter rotation on the ball when you release it, the seam will stabilise (a bit like a gyroscope) and help the swing. Let me explain the grip.

The flat part of your wrist (the ticklish part) needs to be firmly facing the batsman when you release the ball. This helps you keep the seam perfectly upright (top to bottom) then, by varying where the seam points, you can get it to go that way.

You may have the sensation that the ball slides out of your hand slightly, or you may not. Some bowlers report that their fingers turn slightly under the ball on release (if swinging out) or over the ball on release (if swinging in). This is due more to their wrist than anything, but as long as the seam travels down to the batsman without wobbling or scrambling, you're usually in business.

As the new lacquer wears off the ball, you'll be able to shine one side and create a difference in the quality of the two halves. (Yes, cricket is also a game of two halves.) But it is not the shinier side of the two that has a tendency to travel through the air faster, which creates a turning effect through the air. It's about unequal airflows over the ball, created by the seam and surface of the ball that makes the ball change direction seemingly amidships and start to bend along a curved line.

So this is how the newer ball that's been looked after swings traditionally. The ball will swing *away* from the shiny side. Now when you point the seam the way you want the ball to swing as well, you're in for a *real* treat. You simply have no idea just how much it's going to move in the air. Not a clue. It helps to explain why swing bowlers take time to find their line. You'll sometimes see them start off wide of the stumps as they try to make it

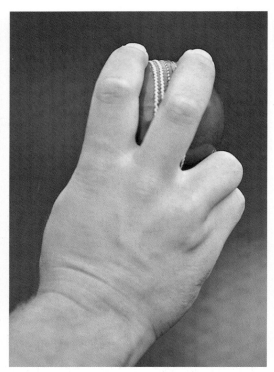

The outswing grip with a new ball. The seam is slightly angled towards the direction you want it to swing and held firmly in the tips of index and middle finger. The wrist is firm and stays firm throughout the delivery action. The 'ticklish' part of the wrist follows the line of the ball.

Seam angled to slip for a right-hand batsman. The outswinger as viewed from behind.

swing. Then they re-adjust and start hitting the 'groove' hopefully. Too much adjustment can see a slight wrist position change and the ball doesn't swing at all. You've probably seen it yourself. The ball ends up going down the leg side as straight as a die. The batsman usually pumps it to the boundary for four and all the fielders moan and groan.

The fun part is then messing around with the seam to find out if it swings more (or less) and so appears that you can swing it later (or earlier) after you've let it go.

Some bowlers are able to swing the ball due to their wrist position alone. The firm wrist mentioned above swings it across their body, whereas an 'eased off' wrist position can tail it back in. This is why we spent so much time at the beginning talking about bowling actions. The purpose is to get your hand into the right position to deliver the ball with pace, accuracy and movement from the wrist and fingers.

Hopefully, you'll be happy to experiment with the release position for yourself. Remember, it's only by exaggerating and experimenting that you'll find out what suits you best. After all, you're unique. And even if you have tried to model yourself on someone else, you'll never be exactly the same as they are.

Just a word here too on angle changes. I could have put this bit anywhere in the book,

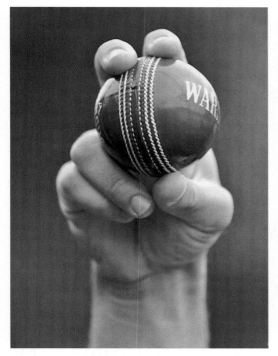

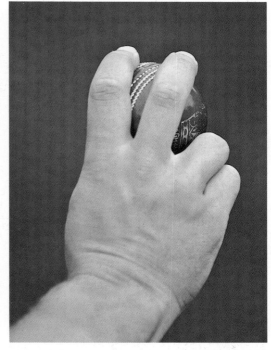

The inswing grip with a new ball. Here the seam is canted slightly in towards a right-hand batsman, showing the way it's going to swing. Again the grip is light but firm. On release of the ball the wrist 'softens' slightly. The sensation is of the fleshy part of the thumb leading the delivery to some extent.

Viewed from behind you can see the seam angle and index finger position. This finger adds a little pressure to the ball on release. The middle finger helps keep the seam upright and balanced.

but as we're talking about how to fool batsmen, let's mention it now.

You can bowl from anywhere you want on the crease. Yet 99.9 percent of bowlers hardly ever vary from where they deliver the ball. If you are very close to the stumps when you bowl – well done. This 'wicket to wicket' delivery is ideal for two reasons. Firstly, you have a great chance of hitting the stumps at the other end if you bowl straight. This means you have a higher chance of LBWs (and umpires love to be in the game so you'll be really popular). Secondly, as there's almost no angle on the ball from your hand to the other end, any sideways movement is maximised.

CHAPTER 8

Awesome Reverse Swing – Your Unfair Advantage

Now why have I only heard of reverse swing recently? It's a question *many* people ask. And the answer is that reverse swing has *always* been with us. It's simply that it took two incredibly talented bowlers, Waqar Younis and Wasim Akram, to bring it to prominent notice. These two Pakistani pacemen pretty much dominated with the phenomenon of reverse swing, as we know it today. They not only terrorised batsmen with speed, but also devastated batting line-ups with late swing, which was nigh on impossible to keep out all day long.

But the grandfather of reverse swing was really Sarfraz Narwaz. Sarfraz was a gentle giant of a fast bowler who played for Northants during the 1970s. He was the first bowler to understand how to bowl reverse swing. It's no surprise then that as a Pakistani Test bowler, he was able to pass on his theories and discoveries to the next generation and beyond. Sarfraz was a clever bowler and, despite not being blessed with blistering pace like Lee or Akhtar, he had great control and accuracy. He was the Glenn McGrath of his day. His legacy quite rightly lives on.

So did the ball reverse swing in previous generations? I would undoubtedly say that the cricket ball has always 'reversed' to some degree. But more recently, in the last couple of decades, bowlers have discovered how to harness reverse swing. Also, there is now an understanding of what state the ball has to be in to make it reverse, which implies that it

was accidental before that. And I would say, yes it was. Many bowlers who swung the ball in one direction were probably amazed when it started swinging in the opposite direction later in the game – even though they weren't holding the ball any differently.

So the first clue about reverse swing is in the condition of the ball. As the ball picks up natural wear and tear, it begins to affect the aerodynamics. And by enhancing the rougher side of the ball, you can accelerate the ball's ability to reverse swing *against* the shiny side. But the key here is ensuring the rough side is as dry as possible.

Darren Gough is one of the world's best exponents of reverse swing. Through trial and error he has perfected the late swinging inswinger during one-day internationals. Now when a batsman is setting himself up to smash an outswinging delivery, it's a bit of a shock when it starts to reverse in the other way. And it's usually bowled pretty full, too.

Conversely, an inswing bowler can reverse swing the ball out, which is disconcerting for the batsman to say the least. If he's a left-handed batsman and the bowler is a right-arm quickie, it is especially difficult to play – something the Australians found out in England during the Ashes in 2005. Reverse swing by the England bowlers was one of the most important differences between the teams. England bowled fast, aggressively and accurately. Australia did not.

There's something worth noting about

the actual cricket ball itself at this point: different types of cricket ball behave differently when it comes to reverse swing. Some take *far longer* to begin reverse swinging than others. However, this ultimately depends on what the conditions are like and how abrasive the pitch is. Dry and dusty conditions will make the ball start to reverse swing much earlier than in greener conditions, or when the surroundings are lush.

The red Dukes ball can take longer to reverse swing than the red Kookaburra ball, which incidentally goes soft very quickly. Having said that, the *white* Kookaburra ball (which is used in one-day internationals and domestic one-day games) swings traditionally and reverse swings the most, both ways. I've always wondered about this and it is baffling. The white cricket ball of all denominations seems to offer more swing than a red ball. Some of us believe it to be because of the number of layers of lacquer on a white ball compared to the red one. I agree with that theory.

But the conditions still remain the *number one* determining factor on how quickly (early in the innings) the ball will reverse swing. That's because it's the state of the ball, for example,

a roughed-up ball on one side, which helps the reverse swing. The ball swings against the shine and in to the stumps thanks to the rough side.

The earliest stage in a game you can expect the ball to reverse swing is not an exact science. In a county cricket game, one cricket ball started to reverse as prematurely as the eleventh over. This is quite amazing. But it does show how pitch conditions can create coarse marks on the leather and irregular and uneven cuts on its surface.

I know that the England management team study this phenomenon very carefully. On certain squares around the country and overseas, you get a feel for when the ball is likely to start reverse swinging, and if you watch the opposition bowlers (if they bowl first) you'll sometimes see the ball 'shaping' in the opposite direction. This means it almost looks as if the ball is trying its hardest to swing, but doesn't quite manage it. So it offers a hint of reverse swing, which tells you a great deal because the ball doesn't suddenly start hooping the opposite way without a few clues first. If you see these clues, it gives you the chance to work on the ball and maximise this extra opportunity.

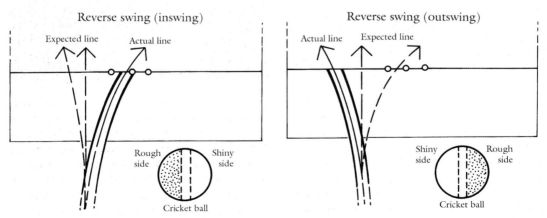

Reverse swing inswing and reverse swing outswing. Experiment with keeping the seam upright or angling it to get the best results.

Over time, and with trial and error, you will come to realise how to get the ball to reverse correctly. And yes, it is an art, which you will absolutely need to work at to master, but the rewards are definitely worth it.

You'll discover that reverse swing is due to the position of the seam at the point of release.

If you class yourself mainly as a right-arm swing bowler with the new ball, you'll probably swing the ball away from the right-handed

batters. This will be your main weapon as it is one of the hardest deliveries to consistently play against. The way to grip the ball is to hold it seam up, but at point of release the ball naturally slides out with the seam angled towards first slip. This is how to get your natural outswing *as well as* the reverse swing.

The conventional way to bowl reverse swing is to polish the shiny side as normal, but more importantly keep the rough side *as*

With one shiny side and one rough side, you have a great chance of reversing the ball. Here, we're all set up for a reverse swing inswinger. It's held exactly like an orthodox outswing delivery to a right-hand batsman, with the shiny side on the leg side. However, this will reverse in the air against the shiny side and into the right hand batsman. The ball should be held as close to the seam as possible (to help eliminate moisture from the fingers getting onto the main part of the dry, rough side).

Set up for the reverse swing, outswing delivery with the shiny side on the off side. By all accounts this should swing in, but the rough side for this state of ball becomes the determining factor, and not the shiny side. Interestingly, as an experiment, we set this grip up with the seam canted slightly towards the reverse swing we wanted. We could have pointed the seam inwards but it still really swung like this. It shows that it is the roughness of the ball, rather than the seam position, that makes the ball reverse swing. So try out the seam position yourself to see what works best for your release point.

dry as possible. A good way to do this is to shine the ball by holding it with two fingers *on* the seam. This way any moisture on your hands will not go on the ball. When bowling reverse swing everything is the reverse of normal swing. That's why if you set up the ball to swing out to the right hander with the shiny side on the leg side the ball will in fact *swing* in to the batsman and vice versa.

Just to be 100 percent clear on this. When the condition of the non-shiny side of the ball deteriorates to such a point that it's rough, you have a great chance of reverse swing. The rough side becomes the side that creates the reverse effect by changing the airflow around the ball. The absolute *must* though, is that the ball is kept very dry. No sweat off the hands.

In a recent county game at Northampton, the ball started to reverse swing for one team but not the other. So much so that on a flat, good batting track, it made a difference to the match result. The bowling side with the reverse swing won the game. It was baffling, as Northampton is one of the grounds conducive to a ball getting into the rough state required. So why was it that only one team managed to reverse swing the ball? Later the answer was discovered.

One of the spin bowlers operating in the middle of the spell, where reversing the ball was likely, kept licking his fingers so he could grip the ball. The dampness got onto the ball and the dry side became neutralised. This habit ended up costing the team an advantage. It shows how delicate the state of reverse swing is and how important it is to understand it.

There's one very big loophole here, which you need to know. Because there will be days when the ball will not swing, either normally *or* reverse, here's something you'll have to try. You will have to think on your feet. You will have to get creative. You will have to be clever. (If you were thinking about bottle tops or scratching the ball illegally, shame on you.)

In one particular game on a notoriously good batting wicket, the bowler saturated one side of the ball with spit and sweat to try and 'weight it' on one side. After a few overs of this, and experimentation with the seam position, the ball reversed inwards and the bowler collected four wickets, all LBW. Now that's very clever.

However, it does go against the 'keeping the ball as dry as possible' instruction earlier. But it is ingenious. And again, I cannot begin to tell you why the ball would reverse swing when it is soaked on one side. Unless it's all about one side of the ball being in such a different state to the other that it turns in the air, perhaps?

Who cares? The main thing is it's *another* way to make the ball reverse – just as long as you don't try to do both versions at the same time.

If you have succeeded in making the ball reverse, then the difficulty batsmen have with playing reverse swing is that the ball swings later. It's almost as if the ball needs three quarters of the pitch length before it realises it's meant to swing. By the time it starts to go, it can be too late for the batsman to do very much about it.

Which is why top batsmen can sometimes try to see what side you have set the ball up in your hand to swing it. That's very sneaky of them. But you can be sneakier. You can try and hide the shine from the batter as much as possible. Glenn McGrath does this sometimes by running up with his non-bowling hand over the ball. And it works.

If you want to perfect the reverse swinging delivery the key is not to try too hard. Instead, attempt to be economical by swinging the ball off a good, probing length. This keeps the pressure on a batsman and will ultimately induce a mistake.

Always realise that your experiences of reverse swing will sometimes be a little hit and miss. You are likely to sometimes get clipped away for four a few times when it doesn't land exactly where you want it to. The same is true of inswinging deliveries in general. My advice is to save the inswinger as a surprise ball and concentrate on swinging it away.

The game plan changes when you bowl to a tail ender. If you swing the ball away from a right-handed tail ender, he'll probably end up playing and missing all night long. It looks mighty impressive. Maybe it causes a few sledges and the odd stare and glance but, in general, most non-batsmen find it harder to edge a delivery than a top player. Why? Because they don't play down the right line usually, or play as straight as a leading batsman.

This is where swinging it back into the stumps works well. If you bowl to hit off stump and the batsman misses it, you're in business. Yes, he might heave you on to the leg side if he's having a swing. But set the field for that and then bowl to hit the stumps with movement from outside off stump. You have a great chance of LBW or bowled. Most tail enders like to get away to the leg side and play, which means they show you all the stumps to hit. And if you are reversing the ball, they probably won't last too long.

CHAPTER 9

Slower Balls – What You Need to Know

One of the greatest achievements of bowlers during the last two decades is 'taking the pace off' the ball. Now that may seem a bit odd to say, when this book is all about how to bowl fast. But knowing how to bowl slower deliveries can be amazingly effective for two reasons.

Firstly, as a defensive mechanism to stop a batsman scoring, it's difficult to time the ball when it's a good deal slower than you expect. Secondly, a slower ball is a great wicket-taking delivery at any time during a match.

A really good quick bowler will have at least one excellent slower ball in his bag. The chances are he'll have two, maybe three he can use at various times. And you'll see them in abundance in one-day matches. That's because it's very hard to set yourself up to strike a ball that has little pace on it relative to the speed of the bowler.

Before we talk about the various types of slower balls, you should know where to bowl them. Slower balls are more effective when they land in the right place and have a greater chance of taking a wicket. A slower ball is a wicket-taking delivery. In my debut for Essex against Somerset, I bowled Viv Richards a dramatic slower ball, which he totally misread and edged through to the keeper. It just shows that even the greatest can be fooled by something so humble.

In a limited-overs situation, you'll find the line for a slower ball changes. If you are bowling with a new ball, or early on, it's best to bowl a slower ball at the stumps. If that seems an obvious thing to say, it's not. Fields are often set for a bowler to bowl outside off stump. So the straight slower ball is about beating the batsman and going on to hit the stumps. The old adage that 'if he misses, you hit', is very true here. And he can chip the ball in the air to a fielder in the ring by mistiming it. So you want him to have to play it by bowling it at the stumps.

However, in the later stages of a limited-overs innings, you don't want to bowl it *too* straight. It's better and more effective to get the ball outside the line of off stump. That's because most batsmen favour the leg side when hitting out. So don't bowl the slower ball 'in the slot' or it will disappear to the tune of *Fly Me To The Moon*. The slower ball outside off stump messes up their timing, the batsman ends up 'fetching' it and can miscue it horribly straight up in the air. You'll see the vast majority of slower balls bowled at the end getting slogged up in the air, which is what you want.

Of course it's all a bit of a lottery. But the unpredictability is what gives you the advantage.

NINE SLOWER BALLS TO HAVE FUN WITH

There's much fun to be had with slower balls. So learning how to bowl them is not only important but enjoyable too. And it really does take time to master them. That's why I suggest you look at the different types of slower ball I've recommended, and try them all for yourself. What you'll find is that some come easily to you. Others will seem impossible. You won't be surprised to know then that practice is the best way to become very good.

They also tend to be the least accurate delivery rather than the most accurate. Why? Because slower balls are notoriously hard to control. Different grips, ball positions in the hand and release positions make for an unusual and, frankly, a 'lottery' approach to line and length. Yet the upside of a slower ball is so rewarding that it's always worth mastering.

Most bowlers I coach can bowl at least one type of slower ball well. The question I have for them is, 'but is that enough?' If you only have one slower ball in your bag, what happens when the batsman works it out? It is extremely difficult to continue to fool batsmen *all* the time with the same slower ball. It's the reason you'll need at least two versions of a slower ball, and I would suggest even three. The great news is that there are many different versions of a slower ball and you can also make up your own. To help, I'm going to show you nine different slower balls.

Some of these are adopted baseball grips used to amazing effect by baseball pitchers in the American major leagues. Others are clever and subtle variations of classic slower balls that have dismissed many of the best batsmen on the planet.

In this book, I'm highlighting the ones I feel are the most effective. These are some of the deliveries that Brett Lee, Shoaib Akhtar, Shane Bond, Glenn McGrath, Mohammed Sami, Freddie Flintoff, Allan Donald, Shaun Pollock, Kapil Dev, Wasim Akram, Malcolm Marshall, Joel Garner, Dennis Lillee, Richard Hadlee and other world greats have used and tried over the years. Naturally, each bowler

has his own version – his own variation on a theme. So I am making the grip and release position of the ball as simplified as possible to help you.

It's always great to copy what some of the world's best bowlers of all time do and have done. But it's even better to do what suits you, because you are the one who's going to be bowling it. My suggestion therefore is to have a go at these different slower balls and persevere with the ones you like. There's no real short cut to bowling them either. You'll have to practise, practise, and practise a bit more.

And if you cannot actually get to bowl them, you can always practise throwing them. By that I mean you get to 'feel' the way the ball comes out of the hand. The fact that you are throwing them for now isn't important. What *does* matter though is the release of the ball from your hand. Get used to it. Try to make it feel as natural as possible. After all, you don't want to give the batsman any clue that you're about to bowl something different.

Let's go through the slower balls one by one now. The fun part is trying them.

One Finger

This is a very subtle variation that takes about 5mph (8km/h) off the speed. It works on the premise that with only one finger, rather than two behind the seam, you don't get as much speed on it.

Grip the ball normally. Then simply slide off your middle finger and rest it on the other two fingers, so you are holding the ball only with your thumb and forefinger. Keep the ball upright when you bowl it. You'll find it's not very easy to control the ball at first, but with practice, you'll be able to master it.

This is a very good slower ball for a set batsman on a good pitch, because it looks like a normal paced delivery. In fact, batsmen I have seen get out to this delivery, often tap down the pitch after being caught at cover or mid off. They think the ball has 'stuck' a little in the pitch and they end up hitting it in the air to a fielder. As I say, it's a subtle one. Just make sure you let fielders know you're bowling it.

Split Finger

This is a variation of a baseball pitch that can work extremely well. The only downside is you do give a bit of a showing to the batsman with your fingers splayed wide on the ball. But it's worth it because the success rates of this one can be very high.

Grip the ball as normal, with the seam upright. Then simply slide your forefinger and middle finger as much as you can towards

the middle of the ball on opposite sides. This creates a large 'V' shape when viewed from behind the ball. The other thing this grip does is to stabilise the ball in flight so it goes down very upright indeed. It's a delivery well used, for example by Glenn McGrath, who hits the seam with more accuracy than most other bowlers by flicking his wrist. As a favoured slower ball for him, he no doubt finds it easy to maintain his precision of line and length.

The wider you spread your fingers, the slower the ball will probably come out. If you can get them very wide, your hand will 'leave the ball behind' as it comes through. However, it has to feel comfortable in your hand and you have to be able to control it.

This delivery is a variation on a baseball pitch. But unlike a baseball, this cricket ball is going to bounce first. So it becomes less

The one-finger slower ball. Grip firmly with index finger and thumb on the seam. Then try to bowl as normally as possible. Make sure you bowl your bowling arm across your body as normal and finish off your action.

The split-finger, slower ball viewed from the front. The wider you spread your fingers, the slower the ball is likely to come out. It's simply a case of spreading your index and middle finger from a normal seamer's grip, to the sides of the ball.

about flight and more about a lack of speed. Having said that, you may also find it does strange things in the air, which all helps.

This type of slower ball can be as much as 10mph (16km/h) slower and has a more dramatic effect. It's still relatively easy for a batsman to see it, but it has a decent success rate – especially in one-day situations. And, if it lands on the seam, it's also likely to dart off the pitch and maybe have even swung before it gets there.

Vulcan Grip

This is a belter. It's my personal favourite because it's very hard to master, which makes it a complete challenge. This is because it goes down to the batsman with hardly any pace on the ball and looks very odd in flight too. In fact, the unusual finger positions on this delivery will confuse the most studious of batsman. If you're a *Star Trek* fan you're just about to find out why this is called the 'Vulcan' grip.

This is as awkward a delivery as you can imagine, in terms of feel in the hand. It works by 'firming up' your wrist. The tendons in the arm that work to have to grip this ball detract from the speed. If you can master it, it's a fun delivery to try and looks extremely unusual.

Keeping the seam upright, hold the ball with the middle finger and ring finger. The

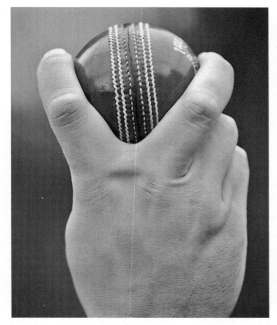

As viewed from behind. You can see the tension in the webbing of the fingers here, demonstrating the amount of 'split' between them. On release, the sensation is that of the ball 'sliding out' of your hand with the sides of your fingers slipping along the shiny leather, thus getting no weight behind the ball.

The Vulcan-grip, slower ball – 'Live Long and Prosper'. The ball is held (as best as possible) between your middle and ring finger, with the thumb supporting the ball underneath. Attempt to bowl this as normally as possible. It's the grip that slows down the ball.

index finger plays absolutely no part in this, which is very unusual. It's also why you'll find it hard to control the ball. And you could experience a tendency to push this delivery down the leg side because your hand wants to 'roll over' the ball from right to left. But stick with it, because if you can control it, you'll really enjoy the lack of pace on the ball.

Set-Back

The 'set-back' delivery is one of the hardest for the batsman to pick up out of the hand. The only noticeable difference is the obvious slower nature of the ball in flight. This is a hard delivery to single out because it's bowled at full speed with no obvious sign that anything untoward is happening.

You simply set the ball back right into the hand. Instead of holding the ball with your finger tips as you would in other normal deliv-

The ball is set back in the palm of your hand. The trick is not to hold it too tight. If you do, you'll find it hard to let go properly. This works because you have no fingers behind the ball to add speed to it. Instead, the ball release feels more like a shot putt because you are almost bowling with the palm of your hand.

eries, you ram the ball deep into the pocket of your index finger and thumb. It almost sits in the webbing of your hand and goes flush against the fleshy pads at the base of your fingers on the top of your palm. The difficulty is to bowl the ball so it doesn't either (a) bounce twice, or (b) land in your half on the pitch.

This is a delivery you have to aim as full as possible. The natural tendency with a ball stuck so far into your grip is to drag it down. If you can get the length right, it leaves the batsman with very few options but to play way too early. Also, it can swing gently with the seam in the right position. That's an added bonus worth experimenting with.

Thumb Off

This is almost the opposite of the set-back delivery because you hold the ball with the fingers – but *only* the fingers – and not the thumb. This sits in the crook of the fingertips to the top of the palm. The ball then rests against the side of your other fingers but no other part of the hand actually makes contact with the ball. You simply tuck the thumb underneath your third and fourth fingers or get it off the ball below it.

When you deliver this ball there is no clue for the batsman. But as you are gripping the ball with your fingers rather than using your fingers to add pace to the ball, you'll discover it doesn't come out very quickly at all. The skill is in landing the ball in the right area. If you do manage that, I'd be surprised if it doesn't completely deceive the best of players. As with some of the other slower balls, you may find the ball wants to swing a little. Practise this one for accuracy and make sure you get the line spot on. There's no point in wasting something this good by not making the batsman play.

Back of Hand

Personally, I find this the hardest slower ball to bowl. Yet others find it easy. But be warned. The delivery and release position are totally alien to any other delivery you'll bowl. This one takes immense practice. The rewards from it are probably the best of all though. I have yet to see a batsman play a well-bowled, 'back-of-hand' delivery, with confidence. If it's bowled short or too full (as with any other slower ball) it will most likely get crashed to the fence. But on target, this is a magical slower ball.

Grip the ball as normal with the seam perfectly upright. As your arm comes over, rotate your hand (so the back of your hand is showing to the batsman rather than the front). You then release the ball slightly from behind your shoulder, instead of directly in front of your head. The trick here is to also flick your wrist towards the batsman at the same time to help keep the trajectory of the ball downwards.

Make no mistake. This is a very hard slower ball to perfect. But because of the back of the hand slowing the ball down and the loop of the ball in flight, it ends up *appearing* to the batsman as if the ball is extremely full of length. I've seen batsmen even duck in antici-pation of the ball being delivered as a beamer, only to find it pitches in front of them before

This grip is all about your index and middle fingers. From the batsman's viewpoint it looks like a normal delivery. But you deliver it by 'ripping' the fingers down the back of the ball without any thumb support. This tends to make it a full delivery, so control is the key.

The knuckles of the bowling hand here end up leading the release of the ball. Make sure you keep the bowling arm high and over the bowling shoulder as you flick the ball from the back of the hand towards the batsman.

trapping them LBW or bowling them.

This delivery also requires you to complete the action as normally as possible to enhance the illusion. The batsman therefore sees the hand and arm come over but the ball is way behind in terms of speed and relative position. It's almost like a *tromp l'oeil*, where it appears to be something it's not. This is one of those extremely special deliveries that, if delivered correctly, can be devastating. Practise it. You will reap the rewards.

Off Break/Leg Break

I have grouped these two types of slower ball together because they are both affected by the fingers and wrist. The off break is probably the easier of the two to bowl. A more natural finger and wrist finish for a fast bowler is across the body and over the top of the ball by cutting down the right-hand side of the ball.

The off break takes pace off the ball, by the fingers and wrist rotating over the top of the ball from left to right at the last minute. It's not about turning the ball (although some really do 'grip' in the surface and turn). It's about a deception of speed. So you can roll the hand straight over the top of the ball. It may even 'kick' a little bit on landing.

The leg break is bowled with the back of the hand turning towards the batsman on release (right to left). It's similar to the back of the hand delivery above, but doesn't need to come from such a high bowling position and is therefore easier to bowl. Also, it's bowled out of the side of the hand, *à la* Shane Warne. Again it doesn't have to turn, and you are not trying to make it do that. However, some slower balls bowled this way do in fact, turn.

Using the Crease

Here's a cheating way to bowl a slower ball. Not cheating in the sense of being illegal,

The release position as viewed from behind the bowler. The hand simply turns from left to right, as if turning a doorknob. It's similar to bowling an off cutter except there's more of a wrist turn rather than just a finger turn. The sensation is that of a karate chop.

The grip is not as important here as the movement of the wrist. The action of the hand is to turn the hand from front to back during delivery. It's very similar to a leg break bowled at speed. Remember, the idea is not to turn the ball but to simply take the pace off the delivery. This happens when you turn the bowling hand through 180 degrees.

but cheating in that it's so easy. This was the delivery I mentioned earlier that Viv Richards didn't spot. Boy was he mad!

The way to bowl this slower ball is to use the back line on the crease as the front line. Surely, it can't be *that* easy? Well, it is. You are now just under a metre further back and therefore a metre slower. And the ball has longer to swing. The only danger you have with this delivery is getting the length right. You have to really try to 'get it up there', otherwise it can fall short.

Have you ever tried to throw darts at a dartboard from twice the distance? It's really hard. The first time you try it you'll be lucky to even *hit* the board. The principle with using the back line of the crease as the front applies here too. You have to think of making the batsman drive at the ball if possible.

Then there's your run-up. You'll need to 'check' it by either chopping your strides slightly or starting from a yard further back. More if you prefer. I've seen bowlers deliver from behind the stumps. My father, who played club cricket for more than sixty years, bowled off spin by using the crease very well. The delivery, bowled from *almost level* with the umpire, brought him a huge amount of wickets in mistimed shots. Remember, as long as the umpire can see you delivering it, it's legal.

Why I like this delivery is that the batsman knows something isn't right about it, but he's not 100 percent sure what it is. He can see something has happened to your run-up (which is off putting too) and the ball just seems to take an age to get to him in relative terms. Yet his brain and reactions cannot stop him from playing the ball as normal. This gives you the advantage.

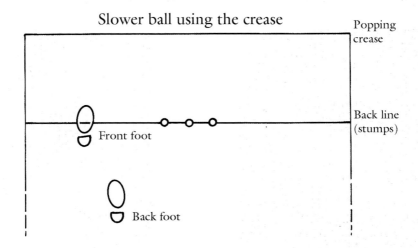

Slower ball using the crease

Popping crease

Back line (stumps)

Front foot

Back foot

Using the crease to bowl a slower ball. The back line level with the stumps becomes your front-foot line. This makes it about a metre slower and longer in flight, too. Both factors seem to draw the batsman in, when delivered on a length.

CHAPTER 10

Yorkers –
The Sand-Shoe Crusher

There's nothing quite like the sight of a batsman totally defeated by a rapid delivery that pitches right at the feet or bat of the batsman. It's either uprooted his stumps or crashed into the toe end of his boot. The toe end of the boot, or sand-shoe crusher, is par-

A Yorker bowled straight at the stumps is a great ball to bowl following something short-pitched. Invariably, the batsman will be on the back foot and be playing over the top of the ball.

ticularly painful. And you have to feel a bit sorry for the batsman as he hobbles off, LBW and nursing a damaged foot. Feel sorry? It's one of the funniest sights in cricket as well as being particularly rewarding.

The thing about a Yorker is that it's so hard to hit. And this makes it a ball to bowl at any time, not just at the end of a game.

Essex played Worcestershire on their way to winning the Tote Sport League in 2005 at Chelmsford. England's Graeme Hick and West Indian Chris Gayle were together building an innings in the middle overs for Worcestershire. It was a key time in the game. Essex captain Ronnie Irani turned to Darren Gough. Within twelve balls he had removed both batsmen with Yorkers – bang, bang.

Bowling a very good Yorker is a minimum requirement for any fast bowler. Bowling a great one can change a match and win it. So this is a skill you need to master without question. But it's not easy. The vast majority of Yorkers, which should pitch right in the block hole of the crease, end up elsewhere. If you miss the block hole, you'll end up bowling a low full toss or a full half volley. Depending upon the state of the game, these deliveries are likely to be dispatched to the boundary by a thankful batsman. And as fast bowlers we hate that.

The truth is, you probably have only 15–30cm (6–12in) of pitch in which to land a good Yorker, split by the popping crease line at the batsman's end. This is where his feet stand.

If you can land the ball where the batsman stands, you'll be bowling perfect Yorkers. But let's get even more precise than that.

How about hitting the laces to the toe area of his boot? Why this area? Because the bat cannot get down unless the feet are out of the way, which of course, they can't. Can you focus in on hitting that area? That's the sort of direction you'll need to make maximum impact and have greatest success.

Rather than bowl in the *general* area of a Yorker length let's get right in on the money. They do in baseball. The pitchers in baseball practise by aiming at a matchbox. Now *that's* precision targeting. If you can hit a matchbox, you can certainly hit the strike zone. And we *definitely* want to do that in cricket terms.

So what should you be aiming at? I am a great believer in looking at exactly where you want to bowl. Therefore, if you follow a line from your eyes to the batsman's foot, it will take you all the way to the base of the stumps, which is your target. If his foot gets in the way, you'll hit his boot between toes and laces, otherwise it will travel all the way to the base of the stumps.

The secret of bowling Yorkers is twofold. The first is mental. You have to simply *know* you are about to bowl a Yorker and then visualise it in your mind before you bowl it. As you run in to bowl it, reinforce that by 'seeing' the ball's flight into the Yorker length. This sets you up perfectly for your brain to compute what's expected. Of course, it happens by a combination of conscious and subconscious thought, which you may not be aware of fully. But that's fine. Simply focus in on the target.

The second secret to bowling Yorkers is less known. It is your bowling shoulder. Your bowling shoulder should drive at the target if you really want to get the ball where it's

The Yorker length

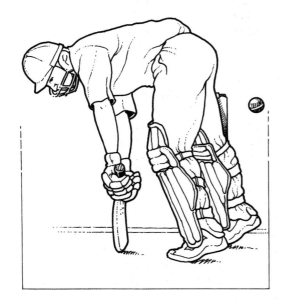

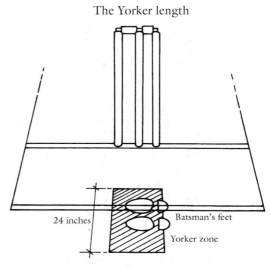

24 inches | Batsman's feet | Yorker zone

An inswinging Yorker from outside off stump and aimed at the boot laces of the batsman is very hard to keep out. Classic signs are the batsman's head toppling over and being off balance when trying to hit the ball.

The Yorker length is about 60cm (24in) deep and 22.5cm (9in) wide. It slightly splits the batsman's crease line, which means he is standing in it. A ball landing in this zone is the hardest delivery to hit.

Chest drive and shoulder drive are key to finding the Yorker zone at the batsman's end. A fuller chest drive leads to a fuller delivery. By driving the shoulder at the target it's easier to power the ball into the zone with pace and accuracy.

meant to be going. In fact, your bowling shoulder dictates just how accurately you bowl any delivery and just how well you can consistently put the ball in the right area. With a Yorker, it becomes vital.

When you drive your bowling shoulder directly at the base of the stumps you also help support the bowling arm to supply a very full delivery, which is exactly what a Yorker is by nature. In addition, it makes it easier to power the ball faster (Yorkers tend

to be quicker deliveries) and drive the chest through your action to help with straight lines and accuracy.

If you don't utilise your shoulder when trying a Yorker you may find it goes down the leg side or ends up as a floaty full toss. So a word of caution here. Don't 'miss' by bowling on the leg side with your Yorker. It's better to be off stump for line purposes (remembering where a batsman's boot lace and toes are when they try to hit the ball) than leg stump, because you have some margin for error in line then.

You can practise by bowling at a tin can (or similar) lined up on off stump rather than a flat object on the ground, because the can is easier to see from 20m (22yd). It also replicates the base of the stumps and you know when you've hit it.

The natural angle of a right-arm over bowler will shape the Yorker in towards middle stump. A left-arm over bowler will shape across a right-hand batsman from middle to off (unless it swings back in, which is a devastating Yorker).

How often should you be trying to bowl the Yorker in match situations? Well, my view is that not enough Yorkers are bowled in matches. They are a great way to burst through a batsman's defence and almost certainly will have a good chance of taking a wicket. Per delivery, a Yorker takes more wickets than any other type of delivery. All you need to ensure is that you have your field set very straight because the batsman is combating the Yorker with a straight bat usually. At best, he's trying to dig it out if it's perfectly bowled. It can mean the ball squirts somewhere unexpected in the field if he does get his bat on it. And if he doesn't, he's out.

CHAPTER 11

Bouncers –
The Head Hunter

This is a wicked delivery, which is why it's so appealing. Along with the Yorker, it's another delivery you should get control of to add to your kit bag of problems for the batsman.

Unlike the Yorker, however, the bouncer is seen by many batsman as a run-scoring opportunity. This is what makes it such an exciting option and a risky one, too. You can genuinely target a batsman who compulsively hooks the bouncer. As long as you set your field as a trap for him, he'll more than likely go after it. This will result in some fast scoring, close shaves or wickets – or a combination of all three.

The other types of batsmen who it's very good to target with the bouncer, are the ones who fend off the short ball. These are players who get their hands very high rather than duck the ball. Chances are they'll pop up a catch to a close fielder. They may even decide it's better to get out towards square leg and bat. That's when the Yorker comes in useful.

The bouncer is not that easy to bowl well. In a similar way to the Yorker, if you get the direction or length wrong it can be ineffective or downright ridiculous. I have seen bowlers think they just have to bang the ball in the middle of the pitch and that's it. But pitch conditions, quality of batsman, speed of delivery and line are other contributing factors as well.

For the purposes of explanation, I am going to assume a hard pitch with a decent amount of bounce and a bowler relatively fast to the batsman he's bowling to (if all that makes sense).

The first thing you need to identify is what *line* to bowl the bouncer. Is it on the stumps, outside off stump or down the leg side? Again, it does slightly depend on the situation and the batsman, but for our example the correct line is over off stump if he hooks, middle and leg stump if he doesn't. Why the difference between the two? If the batsman hooks and wants to take you on, it will be easier for him if you bowl at him so he can use the pace of the ball and 'roll' his shot.

The line to a batsman who hooks is close enough to tempt him, but 'off stump' enough to be hard to control. You want the batsman to top edge the ball or hit it in the air to fielders. He's more likely to do that when he has to 'fetch' the ball slightly.

A batsman who fends the ball off, or who doesn't duck very well, will hate you bowling a bouncer *at* him. That doesn't mean down the leg side though. It means bowling directly at middle and leg so he has no room to get out of the way, either inside the line or outside it.

The key to a real quality bouncer though is the height. What makes a bouncer very hard to deal with is when it's throat height. And bowled straight at a batsman who fends the ball off, this delivery will get him into trouble every time. I am assuming that it's *quick* though. Not a tennis ball bouncer bowled at your own boots so it's on its way down when it reaches the batsman. The one I'm talking about is a searing, rearing delivery about to make another Adam's apple if the batsman doesn't deal with it.

This is the point of a bouncer. It's bowled so the batsman has to deal with it, or negotiate it. The pressure is on him to take evasive action, fend it off or hit it cleanly down. In a game of percentages, it's a high-risk percentage for the batsman.

But what about the batsman who can *really* hook? Should the bouncer be at his throat? As mentioned, the line will be slightly different. And the height must be *at least* throat height. In fact, to some 'happy hookers', you'll want to get the ball head height or above and over off stump. It's a tempter to help them climb into their hook shot. If one or two whistle past their eye line or nose end, it all helps set them up to try something unworthy.

That's got the line sorted out. How do you actually bowl a bouncer? It will be little surprise, since you now understand biomechanics, that this is a ball of maximum pace. So the requirement is in massive shoulder rotation, chest drive and effort. You will basically be attempting to 'bury' your bowling shoulder into the pitch after the ball has gone. Instead of channelling all your momentum towards the batsman, you'll be doing that towards the middle of the pitch. This ensures you can get enough pace into the pitch to get the ball to bounce.

Practise this carefully. It is a different type of follow through as you'll be quite a bit lower on your exit stride than you are usually. Keeping balanced in your follow through will help you achieve success.

In a match situation, it's trial and error to find the exact length you need to get the

A bouncer delivered in the middle of the pitch at speed as the batsman initially considers coming forward.

It rises quickly and is directed at the target – the batsman's head or throat.

ball head high. Plus you'll have to weigh up whether you can get the ball through fast enough so it doesn't turn out to be a glorified long hop. Be aware then that some wickets are simply not made for bouncer warfare. Yet in a strange way this means that the *odd* bouncer can be extremely effective as a surprise weapon. Conversely, on a very bouncy pitch, the bouncer would be expected. A poor bowler would overdo it. Every batsman would be waiting on the back foot to have a go at it.

Clearly, the bouncer is something that is not just about 'letting the batsman have it'. It ought to be part of a well thought out strategy in combination with a correctly set field.

Former West Indian pace bowler Malcolm Marshall, although not very tall, bowled some of the most lethal bouncers of all time. He knew exactly when to bowl them. Amazingly,

he bowled *two* different types of bouncer: one the batsman could hit and one that hit the batsman. He varied his pace on the bouncer to lure people into certain shots and positions then he blasted down a rapid version, which usually ended in a wicket for the bowler or a headache for the batsman.

Another expert in this field was Richard Hadlee. I was fortunate to play in the same team as Richard for two years while at Nottinghamshire. I saw him bowl awesome bouncers the batsmen had dreadful trouble picking up. At first, I didn't know why he caused so many problems with his bouncer. Yes he was quick, but he was renowned for his accuracy over line and length like Glenn McGrath. Batting one day against him in the nets, I realised what it was. He never gave you a clue it was coming. His action never changed

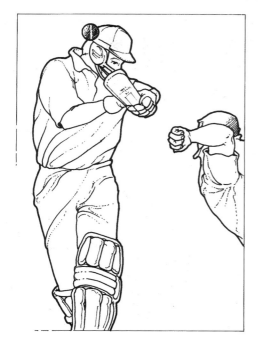

Catching the batsman by surprise, it misses the bat and passes where the batsman's head was. This is an exceptional line to bowl a bouncer as the batsman is forced to either play it or take evasive action.

This is a full chest drive and shoulder rotation into the pitch. A finish like this sets up a bouncer perfectly. The bowler remains balanced and in control whilst utilising his extra pace from finishing off the action.

and he kept looking straight at you. He simply had the ability to whack the ball into the pitch and get it to rear up by bringing his arm over faster on a fuller rotation.

It was mayhem. As a batsman you'd be thinking of coming forward. In a split second, the ball would be zeroing in at your throat. It was one of the best surprise deliveries I have ever seen.

This intelligent use of a weapon is something you should learn to master yourself.

CHAPTER 12

Cross Seam – Deliberate Scrambling

Imagine the pitch is dead flat. Nothing's happening. Here's a grip you can try now and again to make something happen.

It's the cross-seam grip and the aim is to try to hit the seam when the ball lands. Unlikely most of the time when held this way, but dramatic if you can accomplish it. If the ball does manage to hit the seam it might well do something most unexpected, such as rear up. On the other hand, it can miss the seam or hit an

The classic cross-seam grip. This will stop any ball from swinging and turns the bounce of the ball into a lottery. As you deliver this, rip your fingers down the back of the ball to generate a good rotation on the ball.

awkward part of it to keep the ball really low.

I've seen this grip used in a variety of situations and I've seen it work very well. It's bowled as normal except the seam is held across – not up and down – between the fingers. You then 'rip' your fingers down the back of the ball as you release it, causing *counter rotation* to the ball (rotating backwards towards you).

You can be absolutely certain that the line the ball travels along will be gun-barrel straight. That's why it's sometimes used when bowling with a white cricket ball to stop any excess swing. Bowlers use it as a 'control' grip when the ball is simply moving about too much.

I've seen it used for the bouncer grip, in the hope it 'kicks' off the seam. I've also seen it used for the Yorker grip, ensuring it flies arrow-like into the stumps. But it's not really a grip you'd use when the ball is new. That would be a waste.

So this is a grip for an old ball, or a ball you have stopped shining. The odds of you hitting the seam this way are far smaller (because the ball is rotating and it's pot luck if it hits it) but the ball can really jump if you do manage it.

It's additionally a grip you *could* use for bowling a slower ball. Now that would be confusing for a batsman who watches the grip of a bowler carefully – particularly if you mixed your grips up for slower balls as well as the deliveries you bowl with the cross-seam ball.

Bowling is all about getting an advantage in your favour. Use it. Try it. Experiment. It might work.

CHAPTER 13

Bowling No Balls – What's the Point?

You shouldn't bowl no balls. As a fast bowler I bowled no balls like they were going out of fashion and now they have. So I am well qualified to cover them in my book. I can also say that very few coaches know how to stop them happening, which is why I carried on bowling them in my own career. But I am solely responsible for having bowled them.

I used to mark out my run-up then say to the umpire, 'If I overstep the line, will you give me a shout'? It became my opening statement before every spell.

Nevertheless the serious point is that they're really hard to eliminate if you have a habit of bowling them. It's a bit like smoking. You know you shouldn't do it. And you really do want to stop. But you can't help yourself. 'I'll quit tomorrow', or 'Just one last one' if you do happen to bowl a no ball. The worst part is, those who don't bowl no balls (or smoke) cannot understand why those that do, can't stop.

I didn't bowl them all the time – just when I got excited and wanted to get the ball down the other end faster, which was stupid really. Because, the truth about no balls is, that I would have had needed to overstep by a good yard or two to make much of a difference. So if bowling a no ball by a few inches is a complete waste of time and energy then why bowl them at all?

The fact is, whether your foot just touches the front line, cuts the front line half and half, or just manages to keep part of the boot behind the line, there is no real difference to the speed of the ball. As an average-paced fast bowler, you would probably gain 3–4mph relative to the batsman for a yard of overstep. It's just not worth it because you can increase your arm speed with better biomechanics far more than that.

Yet there's a psychological feeling that somehow, if you get even an inch or so closer to the batsman, you'll be quicker. But it's just not true unless your *back* foot is over the front line too. So, it's all in your head. You will not deliberately set out to do it. It's just that your subconscious takes over, adrenalin pumps around your body and the run-up strides get slightly longer. The result? You end up giving the umpire a hard time.

Whilst I'm on the subject of umpires, they *hate* bowlers who are close to bowling no balls all the time. It means they have to look down at the crease the entire time you're bowling. And this can detract from you getting decisions. One club umpire told me that because I bowled fast, by the time he had looked at my front foot then looked up, he couldn't always be sure as to the line of the ball. That's why he rarely gave me LBWs (so he said). It's a serious point. You want the umpire on your side. Give him an easy time. He'd rather spend it giving batsmen out than shouting 'no ball' every over.

Bowling no balls is usually a result of over striding. It could also be that your run-up is wrong and not smooth, so you have an inconsistent stride pattern to the crease. The easy way to get the run-up right is to run it backwards from the front crease line towards the sightscreen then mark it. When you run back the other way towards the stumps, you should find it works. But your aim is to cut the front line with the toe of your boot. Alex Tudor does this very well and rarely, if ever, bowls a no ball. Yet he bowls at 90mph and gets great bounce and movement. By cutting the front line with only the tip of your boot, you have about 22.5cm (9in) of room to play with, which means you can relax. Tudor said his father drummed that into him when he was a child. Good habits learnt early are worth a great deal.

Here's where net practice becomes important. If you bowl from your full run-up, you must always ensure your foot lands correctly during practice. Why? Because you mustn't ever practise bad habits. Yet you'll see bowlers forever bowling no balls in nets. These are the same bowlers who claim they never do it in a match. But it's not worth doing it *at all*. You wouldn't see a long jumper practising foul jumps or a darts player throwing from closer to the board then in a competition. Don't use practice as an excuse to let your standards slip, because that's all they are – excuses.

If you find it hard to keep your foot behind the line, this is where exaggeration comes in. Bring it back a *long* way and start bowling where no part of your boot touches the front line. The back line and the front line are about 1m (4ft) feet apart, which creates a very large box. Get used to that. Start to feel how that is mentally. Then simply land your front foot anywhere in the box without touching any of the lines. It's a huge target and as long as you relax and don't reach for the crease you can do it. Trust yourself to land correctly and simply enjoy the sensation. Bowl like this for ten minutes or so (no batsman at the other end). It's only by constant repetition that you'll convince yourself it's right. Eventually you will settle on this. When you do settle on a new foot landing position, remember to *trust* yourself.

Trusting yourself is important for improvement when the skills are mental–physical. It's almost as though you have to prove it can be successful to yourself first, before you take it on as correct. That's perfectly natural. Bowling no balls, as mentioned earlier, is not deliberate. But it is definitely habit forming. So if you accept bowling no balls as normal, it will be even harder to get out of it. You have no control over extras such as leg byes and byes. But you *do* control no balls and wides. Learn to eliminate them from your game completely if you can through good practice and control. Captains get very frustrated and annoyed if you overstep the front line. Worse still, if you take wickets with no balls you'll get little or no sympathy from anyone. This is a mistake the Aussies made during the 2005 Ashes Test series, and it cost them crucial breakthroughs at vital

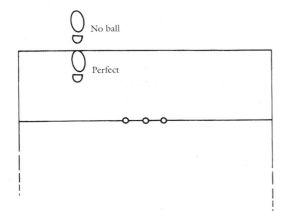

Position 1 is a classic no ball. All the bowler's effort is wasted here. Position 2 is perfect. The tip of the boot is just cutting the front foot line, allowing around 30cm (12in) of room before the umpire gets interested.

times (dropped catches didn't help but that's another issue).

In today's cricket, a no ball is a complete waste of a delivery, so get out of the habit as soon as you can. What's more, extras count in close matches, plus you have to bowl the ball again. In some cricket it counts as two runs and in others it means a free hit next ball. So if you have an issue bowling no balls, take some time out to eliminate them from your game. You can do it in as little as one net session or practice session – if you really want to. And trust me, speaking from bitter experience, you want to.

CHAPTER 14

Accelerated Learning

A decade or so ago, I was introduced to Accelerated Learning through music. At first I was unsure about it. After using music to coach and train with I am convinced of its power. But it is a very specific beat of music that I find works for coaching cricket. And it's backed up by some powerful research, too.

Music performed at 60 beats per minute (bpm) – or one beat a second – seems to have an amazing effect on people. I have two specially written pieces of music about half an hour long that I use as background music when coaching.

These special music pieces, recorded at just the right tempo, activate the left and right brain for maximum learning/retention effect. The music activates the right brain and the activity you are performing or hearing about activates the left brain. This increases the learning potential a minimum of *five times* according to the research. Apparently, listening to 60bpm music accelerates your ability to learn stuff. Why wouldn't you use it?

When your body hears the even, one beat per second of the music, your heart rate and pulse relax to the beat. When you are in this relaxed, but alert state, your mind is able to concentrate more easily. Music corresponds to and affects your physiological conditions. During heavy mental work, your pulse and blood pressure rises, and it's usually more difficult to concentrate in this state. The 60bpm music pieces, especially selected for their beat pattern, reduce your blood pressure and pulse rate and increase your ability to learn at the same time.

As far back as 1993, researchers at the University of California–Irvine reported in *Nature* magazine some results on acoustic enhancements to learning. When college students listened for ten minutes to Mozart's Sonata for Two Pianos in D Major before taking a spatial IQ test, they scored eight to nine points higher than when they listened to a relaxation tape or silence.

In addition, the frequency beat of 60bpm has been found beneficial to brain synchronisation.

It has also been found that music of about 60bpm can change brain waves to the *alpha* range (the brain wave we want to learn faster and retain more information), enhancing alertness and well-being. It has been found that playing music at home, in the office, or in school can help to focus a person. That's why using it in the nets to practise with gives you a head start. If you are daydreaming or unfocused, a little 60bpm music for 10–15 minutes can help to make you more aware and increase your mental organisation.

Alpha brain-wave activity is helpful for sports people seeking peak performance. Recently, sports scientists have shown that increases of alpha brain waves (often in the left side of the brain) precede peak performance. One key difference between novice and élite athletes is in their brain waves. Just before his best free throws, an élite basketball player will produce a burst of alpha on the left side of his brain. Just before their best strokes, élite golfers will produce a burst of alpha in their left brain. Just before their best shots, élite marksmen and archers will produce a burst of alpha in their left brains. Novice and intermediate athletes do not show this alpha pattern.

Creativity is another activity for which alpha is helpful. Scientists have shown that highly creative people have different brain waves from normal and non-creative people (this explains a great deal).

In order to have a creative inspiration your brain needs to be able to generate a big burst of alpha, mostly on the left side of the brain. The brains of creative people can generate these big alpha bursts, and do so when they are faced with problems to solve. Normal and non-creative people do not produce alpha increases when they are faced with problems, and so they cannot come up with creative ideas and solutions.

Any time you have an insight or an inspiration, you know your brain has produced more alpha waves than usual. Increased creativity is helpful for everyone. So getting into the creative alpha state is highly desirable if you want to improve your cricket.

Alpha production is an innate skill of our brains, but one consequence of the modern stressful lifestyle is that we forget how to produce Alpha brain waves. Then we easily fall victim to anxiety and stress situations. Anxiety and stress measurably reduce the strength of our immune systems. People who have more alpha brain waves have less anxiety. Thus having more alpha waves could mean less anxiety and, correspondingly, stronger immune systems, and this is good for everyone. I have found that the 60bpm music relaxes the group taking practice and helps them to focus hard on the new skills they are learning.

So the alpha brain wave indicates a relaxed state of mind – a meditative mind. It is a state of relaxed alertness, good for inspiration and learning facts fast. The left and right brain are said to be working together here. Your mind power increases significantly as the mind then taps into its 'antenna'-like qualities. All of which is exceptionally useful for learning advanced biomechanics.

The music I use is specially written for me. I find that bowlers seem to learn faster, concentrate longer, recall details and facts more easily and are much more focused during difficult or lengthy sessions. I have recommended it to many others who still use it and swear by it. It gives bowlers a definite edge. There are details at the front of the book should you want to know more.

CHAPTER 15

How to Approach Practice

It comes with practice and with the right mindset, a lot of hard work and backing yourself. Hard work is the most important thing; nothing happens without it. If you expect something to happen without putting in the hard work, be it in sport or business, it won't happen. There is no short cut in life and it is something that I know.

Brett Lee

Hands up how many of you go to nets 'just to have a bowl' or 'to turn your arm over'? Well, maybe that isn't how you think, but that's what it ends up becoming.

I would suggest that the vast majority of bowlers rarely practise anything that has much quality or value in nets, which makes nets pretty worthless. Because unless you are working at something, why bother? Also, 'having a few to get loose' isn't very useful either.

You should be trying to work on *something* at practice if you want to improve. So it's worthwhile trying the keys I've shared with you in this book. Presumably you bought this book because you want to improve. That's why, from now on, all your practice sessions must have a purpose. Because you don't just want to run up and bowl. You should be focusing on some part of your game so that you are either grooving it or perfecting it.

But the biggest problem is that there's often a batsman in the net. And he's looking to play as many shots as he can and probably cart the ball everywhere. You end up trying to stop him doing it. It ends up with everyone looking a bit ugly – or at best, ragged.

That's why bowling practice, where possible, should be just bowlers. This is for two reasons. Firstly, you don't worry about impressing anyone or competing with anyone other than yourself. Secondly, you can try things without worrying about where the ball is going. Practice is about *experimenting*. You have to experiment and find out what's possible. You have to make mistakes to improve. You must try new things by changing other things. And if that means breaking the mould, then nets are definitely worthwhile.

When it comes to changes in biomechanics, you'll find out something interesting, too. When you bowl with a ball and then bowl without one, your action definitely changes. I've seen it a great deal with bowlers at all levels. That's because little things going on in your brain alter when a ball is in your hand. You tense up a bit. You get anxious about where the ball's going to go. In other words, you *judge* yourself. And that's harsh, but perfectly natural.

So here's what you can do if you want to make any changes to actions. And this is something very simple but not usually adhered to by coaches or bowlers.

Firstly, make changes in practice without a ball in your hand. Secondly, make them off a very short run-up and by 'walking' them through. I am amazed that bowlers attempt to make alterations to bowling actions without doing these two vitally important things. You cannot seriously change anything unless you break it down into smaller components to give your brain the chance to understand what's happening. Walking through your bowling action works to address that problem immediately. It means learning can begin at once.

The reason for this is that it helps you to make changes in your brain at two different levels – conscious and subconscious. The subconscious is actually in charge even though you may not think it is. Your heart beats, you breathe in and out, and billions of nerve endings and cells work without you consciously having to do a thing.

The process by which the subconscious 'remembers' how to bowl is called *muscle memory*. But this muscle memory takes an average of *ten thousand* repetitions to make a permanent change. It's the reason you need to think about what you're doing constantly. The good news is you can make changes faster when you go through a process of reinforcement. This is the process of discussing what you're doing, showing what you're doing, to others, sharing information and reviewing the processes at the end.

This is a completely new way to learn for cricketers. If you recall the learning preferences of kinaesthetic (feeling), visual (seeing) and auditory (hearing), you'll realise this is a combination of them all.

So it's Discuss, Show, Share and Review

Discuss

Before you can do anything, you need to fully understand what you're doing. This is where you discuss the reason for practising. If you are working with a coach, it's great to sit down and talk about what you are planning to do today in practice. It helps focus your mind and give you a set of goals to achieve. *It's really important you do this.* By discussing the work and purpose of nets, you'll find it far easier to concentrate on them and have a purposeful meaning for net practice.

Show

Showing or being shown what you're about to do is important. When you literally go through the positions you are about to adopt and adapt, it brings them to life. It makes it easier for your conscious mind to cope with change. In other words, it helps reinforce your muscle memory.

Don't ever be afraid to demonstrate what you're practising. In fact, you should do this as much as you can. And if a coach is demonstrating it to you, always make sure you try it too, prior to the actual session. It's easier to be a success when you're learning from your mistakes.

Share

When you share information you have learned, with others, it helps cement it in *your* mind. The act of sharing information means you will have understood large parts of it yourself. Sharing helps boost your confidence. That's because it shows knowledge. And knowledge is power – and the use of it is all-powerful.

Never be afraid to pass on help and tips to others around you as part of the learning process. It's to your own benefit.

Review

Once you have finished your practice, it's time to review it. This could be by way of looking at recorded material, analysis or simply chatting through what's happened at practice. And if this process seems laborious, hearten yourself with the fact that you will improve faster using these methods.

When others give you feedback it's very useful. A third-party viewpoint can often highlight something you've missed – or reinforce the fact you've got things right. It's always worth spending time after your session on this 'debrief' because it is an integral part of your personal development.

It's also a time when you can air your thoughts with coaches, coaches with bowlers, or bowlers with peers who are trying to help. Only by tweaking and constantly monitoring will you find the answer.

This makes for amazing practice and ensures you'll learn far faster than you've ever done before.

CHAPTER 16

Mental Approach – Applying What You've Got

> It looks glamorous, running in, bowling fast, knocking wickets down, but it is a very hard job. It is tough when you get up in the morning, put a foot on the ground and find that everything hurts – heels, knees, ankles, back – and then you have to motivate yourself, tell yourself you can do it.
>
> Waqar Younis

Whenever I've read books about mental approach in sport, they've rarely, if at all, been written by a cricketer. So what? I hear you say. Well, the 'so-what?' factor is that there are some unique challenges associated with cricket. And they are not usually covered by a 'mind expert's' general ramblings. Instead, I am going to ramble generally to see if it makes a difference to you.

This section deals specifically with fast bowlers. It also covers the challenge of being an individual in a team sport. Because let's face it, cricket is merely a series of one-on-one challenges between batsman and bowler. It's a gladiatorial battle to see who cracks first. It is you against him. Your skills pitted against his. Blink first and you lose – that kind of thing.

I think this is what makes cricket similar to many sports yet so different to others. The closest sport for this type of combat mentality is baseball.

A baseball pitcher controls the game. He is 80 percent of the team. The fielders are merely there to deal with the consequences of the pitcher's pitch. In a similar way, the fast bowler has command over a cricket match. Or at least that's the mindset I want you to get into. The game cannot start or continue unless you put it into play. The batsman has little or no idea what you are going to bowl at him. He is reactive. You are proactive. That is your advantage.

If this were a casino, you'd be the 'house'. For example, the house in a casino has a very slight advantage on all bets on the roulette wheel. In cricket, the bowler has that benefit. The batsman usually only gets one chance, because if he makes a mistake he's out. As a bowler you have each and every delivery to get it right. The probability is in your favour.

In the course of a game, several of your deliveries may be 'unplayable'. It simply means that the batsman cannot do anything about them. At all other times, you are inviting the batsman to join in, but you want to control his ability to do so. This is where your accuracy comes in. However, just as important, is your ability to bowl one ball at a time.

Bowling one ball at a time is a mental issue. Imagine you bowl a bad ball that gets hits for four (you'll more than likely still be smarting when you come to deliver the next one), or a batsman runs down the pitch and slogs you over mid-wicket for six. Next time you'll be influenced by what has just happened. And this is the great thing about cricket. It's a series of mind games between batsman and bowler, which is usually won by the person who stays in control of what they're doing.

So the first lesson to be learned here is the 'power of the preceding delivery'. You can use this to set a batsman up. If he's just had a ball whistle past the end of his nose, he's most likely less keen to get right forward to the next ball you bowl. This is when you'd probably get a fuller, faster delivery aimed straight at off stump. Equally, if a batsman has just played an expansive, driving shot through the covers, you might bowl something that *looks* very similar next ball but is, in fact, slightly wider or slower. The aim is to encourage the same shot but with his wicket as the outcome – probably caught unexpectedly (for him at least).

The fact is that as humans we dwell on what has just happened. Our most recent experiences shape the way we respond when it happens again. This is why you can use certain situations to your benefit. When you understand the frustrations a batsman faces: how he's under pressure to score runs, how he doesn't want to get out, how he doesn't want to get hurt by the ball, how he doesn't want to fail – you'll wonder how he ever manages to take any risks at all. Yet take risks he will. Your job is to try and make those mistakes happen more often by the way you bowl.

I heard someone say amusingly about a batting side, that the shock was that they had managed to survive all but ten deliveries. That's why I say a bowler controls the game. As a fast bowler you have the chance to dictate from the start and build pressure on the batsman, without putting yourself under pressure. It's all about your attitude.

Attitude is very important. There is a lot of truth in the old saying that 'your attitude determines your altitude' – what some might call a mindset or way of thinking and seeing the world. Most cricketers at the top have a great attitude and you would expect that. It determines how you apply what you've got. It also affects how well you 'expect' to do – or your ability to have the correct mindset.

Attitude also determines how you feel pressure. And that's an almost intangible thing that can make or break you as a fast bowler. But it's worth remembering that pressure can *only* come from inside. No one can make you feel anything you don't want to. You choose how you feel by how you react or respond. So you can only choose to be aware of your reactions or responses and see them in a new light. In other words, it's how you take action over the situation you're in that determines the pressure. In the vast majority of fast bowlers it often manifests itself as a feeling of nerves.

Not everyone suffers from nerves, but it would be rare if you didn't. Many of the best athletes across a range of sports report at least feeling anxious about performing. Most say it is this feeling of anxiety that helps them to focus, remain sharp and concentrate on the job in hand. Nerves may be your body's way of telling you that you're ready to perform, that the adrenalin is flowing – you can quite literally feel it in your blood.

However you may choose to view this as pressure, and ironically the desire to deal with it only adds to the pressure. By getting anxious and nervous, some bowlers in pressure situations make themselves more nervous, more anxious and this affects their ability to perform. They 'tighten up' and appear almost afraid to perform, or have a fear of failure. Instead, if you understand the response and choose to utilise the adrenalin and trust the skills developed from good practice, you can switch off the self-talk worries about what could go wrong. How about focusing on what can go right for a change? This is where your attitude determines how you cope under stress.

So pressure can be viewed as a good thing you should use rather than be a victim of. That's why pressure plays a big part in the role of a fast bowler. You'll find yourself under pressure in many situations. Your ability to keep positive, remain calm, stay focused and back yourself 100 percent will set you apart from others around you. Sometimes the difference between a fast bowler being average and a fast bowler being exceptional, is attitude. That attitude shows itself when the going gets a little sticky or tough. You can see who's up for a scrap. Those players who relish the burden of performing are often the ones who stand out. And they are certainly key performers you'd rather have in your team than against you.

CREATING AND COPING WITH PRESSURE

Pressure is why I play the game. When it is getting tight you can hear the excitement; the buzz is there and it all builds up well. My philosophy is pretty simple: I just try to bowl every ball where I want to bowl it. And if you can bowl every ball that hits the top of off-stump whenever you want, then you will take a lot of wickets. Even if the batsman hits you for a four or a six, you take the ball and get him out next ball. So all it takes is one delivery to turn things around. I just keep very positive like that.

Glenn McGrath

What is the easiest way to create pressure on a batting side? Wickets. Taking them early and quickly, too. If you can bundle out the top order of any batting team they have virtually nowhere to go. As fast as they can pad up, the next man is coming back to the pavilion. Panic and pandemonium sets in. Batsmen get caught up in the inevitability of losing wickets. They see players come and go. It becomes an irresistible 'critical mass' sensation. They believe they will also fall into the abyss.

What makes it doubly hard is when the fielding side are on top. They are buoyant, chatty, upbeat, maybe even overpowering in the field. Their expectation levels are extremely high. It seems like a self-fulfilling prophecy as the batsmen troop on and troop off. That's what real pressure can do.

The next easiest way to create pressure is by bowling maidens. This is where bowlers hunt in pairs, bowl as a unit and keep the tension going – you're creating a web of tension in the game. It's a delicate dynamic you can almost feel. The scoreboard grinds to a halt. The batsmen can't rotate the strike. They don't look like scoring a run. This type of pressure becomes desperate. The waiting batsmen also get frustrated, which further adds to the feeling of 'we have to do something'. A very tangible sense of anxiety is felt by all the players in these circumstances. When it's in your favour it can be extremely positive. When it's going against you it can be amazingly destructive.

Pressure like this is 'imagined' pressure in the sense that while it appears very real, it's simply how you cope with the situation that makes it easier or hard.

This is what sets apart a great cricketer from an average one in my book. The 2005 Ashes summer saw both Kevin Pieterson and Freddie Flintoff change the course of Test matches when pressure could have caused a weaker character to crumble. By 'standing up and being counted', they both showed the unique quality of applying the aptitude you have to it's fullest. And it's not about whether or not someone has got a huge amount of talent. It's simply about the belief they have in harnessing it.

I often hear coaches talk about a player having character. And it is this character, or moral fibre, that is what it's all about. Without being able to utilise the skills you have in every situation, the less chance of success you are going to have. Can you stay motivated when the opposition is 200–1 chasing 250 as well as you can when they are 100–7? Can you handle external influences such as umpiring decisions, without losing focus? Are you determined to win the game for your side or are you happy to let somebody else do it? And can you deal with sledging on the field?

Sledging is just another way of exerting pressure on the opposition or having it exerted on you. As a fast bowler, sledging is part of cricket today. But don't get me wrong. I am not talking about *abuse*. There is little place for personal abuse, although it does certainly exist, and at times we are all victims or instigators of insults on a cricket field, whether it be name calling, swearing or foul language. However, sledging can be non-verbal or implied. It is about your whole demeanour and attitude towards a batsman or situation.

Some of the greatest fast bowlers 'have a chat' with batsmen while they are bowling. A few of them rarely say anything at all. The great Curtly Ambrose had a withering look, which could weaken even the strongest batsman's heart. Other West Indians, such as Andy Roberts and Michael Holding, had little to say – they let their bowling speak volumes instead. Brett Lee has taken to smiling much of the time. Yet others, like Andre Nel, prefer to be in constant discussion with a batsman over many issues of the day.

You often find that sledging occurs from the need to overcome frustration. And this can come from a batsman too. A form of sledging therefore is a batsman attempting to play a big shot, or hit a bowler off his line and length. It's all about having the upper hand by potentially intimidating the other person. And this in turn is an attempt to create pressure.

Coping with pressure says a great deal about you as a person. You will have a great weight of responsibility as a fast bowler. You're in the team to take wickets – that is your job.

You must be prepared to accept that responsibility when the going is tough. That's why it's a captain's dream to have a bowler put his hand up and ask to bowl in the most difficult of situations. That bowler shows he believes in his own ability.

So do you really want to improve your game and compete with the best? If you do, it will be your attitude of mind that determines how well you improve and perform, or how resilient you can be.

Resilience is a key area for a quality bowler. In other words, how you deal with things when they happen. The act of resilience is possibly the most important quality in a successful player. Resilience in a bowler is to be able to experience an inevitable set-back (dropped catch, batsman hitting a boundary, an umpire's decision, and so on) and almost immediately refocus on the next delivery. It's how well you can 'bounce back' that counts. And it's a mental skill. David Lloyd, former England manager and now Sky Sports commentator, coined the unlikely phrase, 'bouncebackability' when referring to players and teams and their capacity to recover from a set-back. If you have this, you're more likely to be successful. If not, you'll find that when things don't go your way, you falter.

However, when a situation crops up that puts you under pressure, it's very easy to be your own harshest critic. Just as easy is the knack of getting carried away with success. Both of these things help you to lose focus by either beating yourself up or allowing euphoria to take a hold.

Try not to get caught up in self-criticism or, for that matter, self-congratulations. Your aim is to stay in the 'flow of a game' by continually moving forward mentally and responding to it as it happens. What has gone before quickly gets stored as experience. The secret though is to not take a bad experience as regret or worry. Realise that what happens ahead is an immediate reaction to the circumstances that are unfolding. This means you simply deal with the events *as* they take place. You have a balanced mental state, unaffected by proceedings around you. However, it's hard to keep a level head regardless of the situation. If you can achieve it you'll have a significant advantage.

Understand how your mind-body reaction state takes place. More importantly, realise that you can deliberately alter or control this by how you think about it. *You* control your own thoughts and reactions. The ability to do this is called self-regulation.

The goal of self-regulation is to recognise that when you are under pressure (which is usually a stressing or tightening experience), you can handle it. So part of the solution is to understand *how* this can be controlled. Most top cricketers have some strategies that they have utilised over the course of their experience to calm down or psych up. However, very few of these cricketers have learned to do this in a methodical manner with clear knowledge of how to make them work in competitive situations. Yet the good news is this ability can be taught to nearly every person. You can take it into matches and make it work for you.

Recognise there is a natural preference, when something goes wrong, to attempt to solve it by what becomes a counter productive response. And if you're like 99 percent of fast bowlers, your reaction will probably be to try harder. This can have negative consequences as well though. For example, you can try *too* hard, which seems an odd thing to say, but is a fact.

Trying harder usually means putting *more* pressure and demands on yourself in order to correct the problem. Ironically, this increases the tension or anxiety response that is the culprit in preventing you from getting back to using your natural ability. To illustrate this in a simplistic way think of the example of a rubber band.

A rubber band has considerable elasticity and flexibility. If you hold the rubber band with a minimum amount of firmness between two fingers you will note that you can move it around quite easily. You can change its direction and push it this way and that. However, if you pull the rubber band, creating more tightness, the tension goes up and the rubber band has far less control.

That is fine if you want to snap someone hard, inflicting injury, but not good for a more fine-tuned response. And as a fast bowler you'll want fine-tuned responses that you can control. The skill is not to try to solve the problem by working harder, stretching tighter, and thinking more. Instead, relax more, trust your instincts, and return to a more natural comfort zone of performance. You are not forcing the ball at the batsman. You are searching for timing, effortlessness, rhythm, ease and freedom of movement.

Besides understanding this concept, there are some other examples from other sports of trying too hard. In golf, for example, to reduce 'white knuckle grip' (holding the club too tightly, preventing the player from 'feeling' the shot) the player imagines the golf club grip as an eggshell, which must be held with a certain looseness to prevent it from breaking. This helps you stop the mental response or thinking process that creates the tension.

There are several strategies that can be used for stopping unwelcome thoughts. One is the use of positive affirmations – self-statements that immediately replace negative ideas with positive ones. 'I am a great fast bowler', 'I am strong, I am capable'. Another, when becoming initially aware of some tension, is to use focus and relax commands, 'I am calm', 'I can relax'. Use a personal mantra, a word or phrase that serves as a reminder to stay in the moment.

Find some of your own you feel comfortable with. When you feel the pressure or tension building, simply repeat them to your-self mentally as triggers to help you retain self-control. They really do work.

THE POWER OF THE MIND – FAKE IT 'TIL YOU MAKE IT

Some cricketers, when they first come across this whole concept of the power of the mind helping their career, don't buy into it. Sure, they know that having the right attitude would help, but to suggest you could get maximum performance by tweaking your thoughts comes across to some as just a little strange. The very idea that by repeating something in the mind, over and over, would actually help performance seems initially ludicrous. Unless of course, you already know how powerful your mind and belief systems are.

So I'm going to introduce you to the won-derful phrase, 'fake it 'til you make it'. It's a short-term answer, rather than a long-term solution, but it can help.

At first, you may not have a clue what benefit this whole mental concept could pos-sible have. After all, how can you pretend you are something you are not? Wouldn't you just be conning yourself by telling yourself you could do something or achieve something even if you doubted it or maybe thought you weren't able to succeed at it?

The answer is, 'yes', and that's the *entire* point. The human mind is like a fertile piece of land. Whatever you plant in it grows like crazy. You can fill it with rubbish and it will grow rubbish. You can plant negative thoughts and you will become a negative person. You can also think about what can go right and remain optimistic. The fact is your mind doesn't care what you plant, but it will absolutely, 100 per-cent of the time, grow what you sow. So you'd imagine then that we are obviously spending all of our waking moments filling our heads with thoughts, ideas and beliefs that bring out the best – that we're constantly consider-ing the possibilities, seeing the good, concen-trating on a positive outcome to all situations. Of course we're not.

As humans, we find ourselves thinking about things that may never happen, things that can go wrong, or things that are inher-ently negative. Why? Because it is a lot easier to imagine the worst or at least expect it. That's because we're *conditioned* to talk about and think about bad news rather than good. The newspapers, TV, radio and all forms of media are filled with disasters, deaths, trag-edies and things that go wrong. These are the very things that fill our heads every day. If you want to be depressed, watch the latest news. There's rarely an uplifting story on there.

As you chat to others, you realise that some people constantly moan about this or that, criticise something or someone, or gen-erally find things that are not right with the world. You'll recognise the language. People say simple things like, 'I'm never lucky', or 'every time I do such and such it goes wrong'. Never ask certain people how they are feeling in case they *actually* tell you. Then you can be depressed with them. Many people are nega-tive, critical, judgemental and fault-finding. It's just the way some people are.

So we live in a world where many people are taking on board the things they think about from a position of 'lack' and non-achievement. That means if we are conditioned to find a hundred reasons why we can't do something or we are used to thinking only about what might go wrong, we have to change that habit.

Your mind doesn't care *at all* what thoughts you fill it with. It will nurture those and help you achieve the aims, whether they are good or bad. Why then fill your head with nega-tive thoughts? Yet many people take on board all the very worst things they hear. They then think about them, mull them over and then wonder why they are sceptical, pessimistic, downbeat or doubtful about their chances of succeeding.

Here's where 'fake it 'til you make it' comes in. The trick is to 'talk up' what you can achieve, in your mind. If you want to become a great fast bowler, you have to act like one. You have to start doing the things that a great fast bowler would do and begin telling yourself (not others) the positive thoughts about yourself.

Everything about you – your behaviour, the way you practise, your presence, your attitude of mind and your belief system – has to reflect the bowler you want to become, but you must mentally do it *before* you are that person. When you start to take on the persona of a great fast bowler, your mind begins to accept the end goal as the target. It then seeks to find ways to help you achieve the goals that are in your thought system.

You might have to genuinely fool your mind by repeatedly telling it over and over how good you are. This might make you feel a bit uncomfortable if you don't actually believe what you are saying. But it *doesn't matter* whether you believe it or not at the beginning. All that matters is you tell yourself, quietly, repetitively, what you want to achieve and who you want to become.

The mere act of repetition of thought imprints the feelings as real. Regardless of resistance initially from your 'negative barriers', you will start to recall the positive beliefs and emotions to change your entire behaviour towards yourself.

Always put your positive thoughts and feelings into the 'now'. What I mean by that is don't say 'I will become', but rather say 'I am', or 'I have'. The reason is simple. In the subconscious mind there is no past, present or future. If you don't say it as 'now' your mind cannot start.

I'm asking you to think about what you want and say it to yourself as if you already have it. Imagine how you would feel to actually have the skills and talents you dream of? Now tell your mind you have them immediately. Imagine you are already the person you wish to become.

Confidence and arrogance in sport have a very fine line dividing them. That's why any positive thoughts of your cricket success should be kept in your own mind. However, if you are self-confident you are more likely to try new things and be open minded to making changes. The aim of this book is to help you get there. It's time to help yourself control the power you have inside your head.

WHAT TO DO WHEN YOU HAVE A BAD DAY AT THE OFFICE

It's going to happen. The day when everything you try goes wrong. But how you cope with a 'bad day at the office' in cricket terms is dictated a great deal by your ability to be rational.

Earlier we touched on attitude and coping with stress and pressure. Well, when you have a bad day the realisation of all your fears has probably come true. In the moment of that bad result or bad experience, the way you deal with the reality of it is crucial. Why? Because it impacts on your performance either during the game or for the next match. Carrying mental scars is something we all do but you need to learn how to overcome them.

I have been in many situations where things didn't go right. And when this happens there's a blame culture. It's not an intentional blame culture of course, but you know that your team mates are disappointed. If your ragged performance has led to a defeat you cannot hide from the fact that you have contributed to the loss. And it *really* hurts. But understand that the vast majority of people are more interested in their own performances. The team might lose, but if you've scored a hundred or taken a hatful of wickets in the process there's personal pride and achievement in what you've done. The opposite is true in victory for the team following a very bad day for you.

I always hear cricketers say that it's the team that counts, which is true. Yet I don't know of one cricketer who isn't interested in their statistics, their averages or their performances, rather than those of the team. So let's be brutally honest about this, having a bad day is horrid. And despite what players say, it's their own accomplishment that is important to them.

The worst day is therefore where your performance has led directly to defeat. It is just as hard to deal with having a nightmare whilst the game is going on. Your performance is poor, you're bowling badly and you don't want to carry on but you know you have to. However, it can be overcome by backing yourself regardless of the outcome. This takes a strong belief and a positive outlook. It also takes into account that you *will* have days that go wrong. It's all part of the game. Recognise that fact and don't let it bother you.

It's never easy to be philosophical about things that go wrong. But it's only the *way* you take on board the information that makes it depressing. Therefore it's all about perspective.

When two teams meet, one side wins, the other loses. The winning team has a totally different perspective on the result than the losing team, yet the physical outcome hasn't changed. What has altered is the way the result has been taken on by each set of players. In a similar way, two boxers have completely contradictory viewpoints over their performance. Yet what is different between the two is the way they interpret the result.

That's why people like Duncan Fletcher impress me. The England coach is one of the most level-headed people you could ever wish to meet. He's quiet, unassuming and gets on with the job in hand. He looks exactly the same whether England wins or loses. Even on winning the 2005 Ashes, he didn't show any emotion when being interviewed. Here's a man who understands how to treat adversity and glory as equal impostors.

My own personal ethos in any situation is to take out what is positive. A difficult or challenging situation presents an opportunity to turn it around the other way, and the solving of it brings even greater feelings of achievement. Anyone can be negative. But the skill is in working out why something has happened and learning from it.

If you've made mistakes, you're one mistake closer to getting it right. The easiest thing to do is to throw all your toys out of the cot. However, it's far harder to take it on the chin and come back stronger. This is the reason so many people cannot accept criticism. Being able to take criticism from others (and yourself) and use it positively is a skill that's worth learning. People usually see us very differently from how we see ourselves, and that's often why we view criticism as unfair or unjust. But we may have seen the same thing as they did if we had looked at ourselves through their eyes.

I was always told to listen to everyone who had advice for me and take out the bits that I needed. But what if you don't know what you need? Or what if you don't know what bits to take out? Advice can affect players badly. I know of a few cricketers who allow themselves to be influenced by everything they hear. When this happens they take on all kinds of theories, ideas and excuses for non-performing. What happens then is that the advice becomes the safety blanket rather than what they know and understand about the game. When you are under the stress of performing, you always revert to what you know. It's not wrong to take on board advice – in fact you have to. Just look for the parts of it that suit your game, not someone else's. And remember that the basics are the basics, however good or bad you are.

This brings me full circle to how to cope with a bad day. You have to be even handed about it. Acknowledge mistakes if you've made them. Give credit to the opposition or rivals, if they have done well. That's only fair. It takes a big man to truly thank the opposition for the game, after they've wiped the floor with you. For me, Brett Lee is a shining light in this field. He's one of the first to shake hands, put his arm around people and have a beer with the winners. Yet on the field, he's just about ready to take your head off. Brett Lee and other world-class players understand that giving praise and accepting criticism is what turns an ordinary cricketer into a human being.

Be humble. And be grateful that others care enough about you to want you to perform better. A bad day at the office is all about perspective.

CHAPTER 17

Twelve Things You Never Knew About Fast Bowling

1. To bowl with accuracy, throw your bowling shoulder at the target as you deliver. You can also use this for throwing accuracy too.
2. If your mechanics are correct, your run-up is likely to only account for about 10 percent of your overall speed.
3. Allowing for variables such as arm actions, delivery stride lengths, back-foot and front-foot positions and so on, there are 2,592 different combinations of legal bowling actions.
4. The average 1st XI club bowler bowls at between 70 and 77mph (112–120km/h).
5. The ball slows down by around 15 percent from leaving the bowler's hand to then pitching and reaching the batsman (dependent upon pitch conditions).
6. There is no such thing as 'good areas'. There is only one area to bowl and it's usually aimed to hit the top of off stump.
7. A slower ball at the beginning of a match is bowled straight, whereas during a late run chase it's bowled wider. The reason is that the batsman will 'fetch' a wider ball, increasing the chances of mistiming it and skewing it skywards for a catch.
8. Malcolm Marshall was the first bowler to bowl two different speeds of bouncer on purpose. The first one (slower) was to encourage the batsman to hit it. The second one (faster) usually ended up hitting the batsman.
9. Fast bowlers are *made* not *born*. This is not to say that everyone can bowl fast. It's how you apply what you've got that counts. Some of the most unlikely fast bowling prospects have developed into true quick bowlers, whilst others have suddenly gone from medium pace to fast by learning the secrets of the action.
10. The maximum allowable bend in the bowling arm on delivery is 15 degrees. Tests prove that by walking up six paces and throwing the ball with this degree of bend in the arm, speeds of over 90mph (144km/h) are possible.
11. Left-arm bowlers are less likely to bowl as fast as right-arm bowlers due to feet set-up in the crease and 'shutting off' their actions. There is no physical reason why left-arm bowlers set their actions up this way, so it's a mental issue.
12. A slower ball is less accurate than a faster one. It's far harder to bowl a slower ball where you want it to go because of the change in biomechanics that go with it. A quicker delivery is usually a result of getting everything lined up correctly.

CHAPTER 18

Ten Legal Tricks to Fool the Batsman

1. Run up with your non-bowling hand covering the ball. It looks odd and disguises what you are about to bowl. It gets the batsman thinking you are trying to cover something up even if you are not.

2. Don't use your non-bowling arm in the delivery action. Keep it by your side. Darren Gough has used this delivery on occasions to baffle the batsman and put him off.

3. Wear a dark sweatband on your non-bowling wrist. It's not easy to get away with this. The cricket ball is red and the darker colour helps distract the batsman's eye for a split second as you load up to bowl. The umpires may or may have something to say about it, so use your discretion. But it's worth a go.

4. Make good use of the crease. By bowling one ball from the stumps and the other from way out on the crease, the angle of delivery can be altered by up to 12 degrees. This can be the difference between finding the edge or not, and can also create doubt in a batsman's mind.

5. Related to the above, use round-the-wicket tactics to completely change angles – particularly to a left-hander. Flintoff did this to Gilchrist during the 2005 Ashes summer and won the battle. It can also be effective for a few overs against a right-hand batsman to mess up his interpretation of line.

6. Keep a new batsman waiting as long as you can. Use delaying tactics and field changes to help build up pressure on him. A fresh batsman at the crease simply wants to get on with it and feel the ball on bat. Take time to set the field right, saying things in a loud voice, such as 'can you come in here for the one that pops?', or 'as it's moving so much we need another catcher in here'. And also point a lot.

7. By putting a fielder in a batsman's eye line you can put him off. England has used the tactic well for straight fielders almost next to the pitch, on 'the drive'. It can be for specific threat or as a spoiling tactic. The batsman can see the fielder and has the overwhelming urge to move him, usually by forcing a change in the field. It works well when not much is happening in the game, because the batsman wonders why you have suddenly done it.

8. The use of the 'three-card trick'. This is where you set a certain field, deliberately deploying fielders in catching positions to make the batsman 'think' he's going to get a particular type of delivery. Then you bowl something quite different. Or you can 'set up' a batsman with two deliveries he expects, and then one he doesn't. This works because of the power of the 'preceding delivery' syndrome.

9. Reverse swing. Learn this one as best you can and use it to great effect. The vast

majority of batsmen cannot spot it and are not expecting it. And because you set up just like conventional swing, even the most seasoned international finds it difficult to cope with.

10. Learn to bowl at your own rhythm and not that of the batsman. A batsman scoring freely really cannot wait to face the next ball. Conversely, a team under pressure to score quickly doesn't want the overs to go by too fast. If you are dictating the pace of the game in the field, you have more chance of controlling the match in your favour. Learn to slow down and speed up accordingly. When a batting side is struggling, the last thing they want is a rat-a-tat-tat of overs before they know it.

CHAPTER 19

The Prevention of Injury in Fast Bowlers

This is the technical bit about how to avoid injuries when bowling. I make no apologies about that. But I do ask you to stick with it and read it. When you understand, or at least begin to find out about how to protect yourself, you'll have the chance of a longer career.

Much emphasis has been put on injury prevention in fast bowlers and with good reason. You can't play if you are on the physiotherapist's table. Also, bowlers with actions that are *likely* to cause injury are corrected. This didn't happen twenty years ago. So why is it that the incidents of injuries seem to be higher than ever?

One theory is that the reporting and diagnosis of injury is far better now. I would go along with that to a large degree. We are able to monitor injury and predict it easier than before.

The demands of fast bowling place a great deal of stress on the cricketer. As a fast bowler you will be expected to perform in bursts of intense activity within the course of a game. This can be anything from a match spanning an afternoon, one day, or up to five days. The principles in the prevention of injury involve the promotion of strength, endurance, flexibility and nutrition, all of which are the general components required to maintain health. You'll need to read this if you want a solid framework to help you stay healthy.

EXERCISES AND TRAINING

If a person wants to bowl at 95mph consistently, he is going to be strong through his abdomen, his muscles. Without being too big, he has to be very fit and have a very healthy lifestyle.

Brett Lee

Before you read this and the following sections, please note that many of the exercises mentioned here are quite advanced and the schedules mentioned would be those of a conditioned fast bowler with time to train. This section merely gives you a flavour of the type of training a professional or highly evolved fast bowler might embark on. My strong recommendation is that you always seek the advise of a health-care professional before you embark on any physical activity. You should also work with only qualified coaches and trainers who can guide you through the process of exercising. The whole point of training is to keep you on the pitch longer and help you perform better. So don't abuse it or take it lightly.

You'll also find *some* examples of the types of exercises relevant to each section. This book is about fast bowling primarily and better qualified people than me can advise you on what exercises to embark on, based on your current fitness levels. Therefore, use this book as a creative resource to inspire you to do your own detective work.

Fast bowling is a highly complex blend of power and poise, strength and balance, flexibility and suppleness. There is no 'one size fits all' routine of training methods and exercises that work for everyone, because no two people are alike.

However, the physical side of fast bowling is important. Put another way, being able to master the physical side of fast bowling is an *absolute necessity*. Poor fitness and muscular strength will result in inaccurate bowling, a high risk of injury and the inability to recover after matches.

Fast bowling is a unique combination of explosive energy and stamina. You need to be able to perform in short, sharp bursts, or maybe over longer, more controlled spells. You'll need a blend of aerobic and anaerobic training, speed and strength work, and flexibility and stretching drills to help get your body in the right shape to support your action.

As a fast bowler, you should consider the following areas of exercise: aerobic training (for stamina); speed work (for explosive force); strength work (to increase your muscle power); Pilates (for core stability) and yoga (for flexibility). Many of these areas cross over. You'll find that by doing one set of exercises for example, you'll be helping in other key areas.

If you have access to a gym or health club that would be ideal, as you can organise your own space and work there. The key here is to have a routine and stick to it. Far too many fast bowlers 'have a go' at getting fit and improving their physical side of cricket, but do not master it. Even at International level, bowlers are sometimes guilty of not maintaining a high enough level of fitness and strength. It can mean the difference between a talented bowler becoming a great fast bowler or not quite making it.

I am assuming that, as you have bought this book and discovered the secrets of how to bowl fast and straight, you want to be the best you can be. This part is the workload that goes with achieving your goals. It would be a shame to have your physical attributes let down your ability to bowl.

I also recommend that you find out more about the cross-training activities and exercises that go towards building strength, stamina, speed and flexibility. There are excellent resources on the Internet to get you started, or ask a personal trainer for guidance and take it from there.

Below are a variety of bits and pieces to get you mentally stimulated. They're taken from a section of my favourite training schedules from world-class bowlers, élite-level athletes and renowned fitness trainers, coaches and heath-care professionals. Read them for interest purposes. If you want to start a fitness regime, only do it under guidance.

GENERAL PRINCIPLES OF TRAINING OVER THE SEASON

Cricketers are increasingly facing a greater number of games, as the format of the sport changes. Firstly, there's the introduction of Twenty20 cricket for clubs and counties, and the proposed reintroduction of a shortened version of the game at school level. This leads to the temptation to have a more aggressive style of play (it used to be called slogging). It is essential, therefore, that whatever level you play at you have a sound basis of how to train and also when to rest.

Periodisation

Periodisation is the term given to the division of training into three phases over the course of a season. It consists of conditioning, pre-season and season phases.

During the conditioning phase, training comprises both aerobic and anaerobic training. In a normal cricket season in the United Kingdom this phase would usually last from the end of the season in September through to January. You will be training intensely to the extent that you will feel consistently tired. After this, from January to April, you should switch from pure conditioning to more emphasis on technique and skills.

During the season phase you will maintain basic fitness with focus on competitive performance. It is your ability to maintain good skills that's important here. To allow complete recovery from one season to the next, a period of between four to six weeks should be allowed, free from vigorous training. The term 'active rest' is often used. This comprises of activities such as swimming and cycling thereby using other muscle groups than those used in competition.

It would be wrong to use the training schedule of a successful international cricketer in the hope that their regime would be a template for your own body. Different people respond to the stress of exercise at different rates. This is determined by the specific training stimuli, recovery time, psychological make-up and the nutrition of the fast bowler. And unless you yourself are at that level, your own schedules are likely to be completely different.

In general, it takes four to six weeks for the nervous system to adapt, thereby improving performance. After this, there are changes within the muscle itself. So it's not a quick fix.

Table Framework for Commencing Fast-Bowling Training

Week	1	2	3
Monday	Jogging Weight training	Jogging Weight training	Jogging Light weights Bench presses
Tuesday	Interval runs (4 × 120m)	Interval runs (6 × 120m) Plyometrics Bowling technique	Interval runs (3 × 150m) timed Bowling technique
Wednesday	Jogging Weight training	Jogging Weight training	Jogging Light weights – clean and jerk
Thursday	Interval runs (4 × 200m)	Interval runs (400m–300m–200m–100m)	Interval runs (1 × 300m) timed
Friday	Plyometrics Jogging Weight training	Bowling technique Jogging Weight training	Bowling technique Yoga Jogging
Saturday	Interval training (6 × 100m)	Interval runs (4 × 200m)	Interval runs (6 × 20m)
Sunday	Active rest, e.g walking	Active rest, e.g swimming	Active rest, e.g cycling

The magnitude of the training stimuli will be determined by a sound understanding of the concept of overload. Overload involves stress being applied over and above that usually encountered (so you push yourself harder and longer). Provided that this is not too intense or frequent then the body will undergo 'super-compensation' during periods of rest in between exercise.

Training can be increased by raising volume or intensity. The volume of the work is determined by the duration of the workout and the intensity refers to the quality of the exercise session. In general, the training should be increased by upping the volume before raising the intensity.

Your training will be specific to the demands imposed by fast bowling. This will require training suited to short sprints with an explosive release of energy in the delivery stride. Therefore it would be senseless for the fast bowler to perform jogging longer than three miles as this will not aid in the objective of explosive sprinting. You require pace in the run-up, an explosive release of energy in the delivery stride, flexibility and stability in the delivery stride that allow the accurate release of the ball, and a coordinated follow through, maintaining momentum through the popping crease.

To help, refer to the framework that an élite-level fast bowler might use to begin preparation (*see* page 108).

The purpose of jogging is to increase the endurance of the cricketer. This form of training is aerobic, whereby the body uses the sugar stores for energy. There are complicated ways of measuring aerobic capacity in the laboratory setting, which are not important here.

For our purposes, a reliable method is to predict the aerobic capacity by measuring the heart rate at a specific workload. This is commonly performed at fitness centres. As a guide, you will initially be working at between 60 and 75 percent of your maximum heart rate. As you get fitter, this capacity increases and you can train at a higher rate before you go into the anaerobic phase.

After a period of training, as described in the table, you should undertake 10–15 minutes of milder activity. This is thought to reduce the degree of muscle soreness and stiffness. Gentle stretching of the muscles used in the session of training will assist the warm-down process.

During a match situation, the period of time spent in between bowling spells poses some real dilemmas. It is tempting to stop activity completely, often hidden in the depths of the outfield.

However, this time should be utilised to keep the major muscle groups active. The degree of energy you spend doing this will depend on the match situation. If your captain is demanding a match-winning effort over six overs, you should keep circling your arms and perform small 10m shuttle runs as the ball is returned to the other bowler after it has gone dead. The purpose of this is to keep the temperature high, and therefore the metabolic rate of the muscles high also.

Recovery After Exercise

As well as the warm-down you should pay as much attention to the recovery period as that paid to the training sessions. In the conditioning phase of the training cycle you are particularly prone to fatigue. If this happens the training load can be reduced and you can recover more easily. It is tempting to blame the fatigue on being 'unfit' and increase the training workload, thereby carrying on a vicious cycle. This will lead to an 'over-training syndrome' where you feel persistently tired, feel depressed and will under-perform over a period of at least two weeks, despite rest.

More than 90 percent of sufferers will complain of poor sleep patterns, including difficulty getting to sleep, sometimes very active dreams or nightmares and awakening unrefreshed. There are no reliable ways of predicting who is prone to this over-training, but there are some warning signs that may be detected by using a training diary on a daily basis. The diary will include a record of all training sessions, rest days, sleep pattern, mood, and morning resting pulse. Training should be reduced if you report a low mood or if the heart rate increases on successive mornings. Please bear these things in mind, as they are important and easily overlooked.

Hard training will produce increased tone in the exercised muscles. This increased tone may impair the delivery of nutrients to the muscles and slow the removal of metabolites. The increased tone reduces the elastic properties of the muscle and therefore its ability to absorb shock. The tissue is more likely to become strained and injured. This micro injury will cause scar tissue, which in turn is also less elastic and hampers force transmission through the muscle. Eventually this scar tissue will stick to other muscle fibres, decreasing muscle performance over the long term. Massage is thought to prevent this cycle by reducing the tone of the muscles after exercise, allowing increased delivery of nutrients. The massage therapist will detect muscular trigger points and treat them.

The amount of sleep required during a training programme should never be underestimated. Often as much as 10–12 hours of sleep will be required to allow recovery of the body. So if you enjoy your bed, you'll love these figures.

Juggling a full-time job, time to eat healthily, time to exercise, enough sleep and a social life will be difficult. Athletes in other fields of sport take a nap in the afternoon. (I work with one fast bowler who always sleeps between 4pm and 6pm when not playing.)

When athletes become very fatigued they are often advised to sleep as long as is necessary, sometimes spending almost the entire weekend in bed, sleeping as much as possible. It is during sleep that hormones such as growth hormones are released, helping tissue to repair and heal. The sacrifice of sleep will lead to longer-term problems, such as the over-training syndrome.

Nutrition is important in order to replenish the used stores of energy after exercise and help muscle and bone to heal, as well as to provide rehydration. There are three major components to replenishing stores: carbohydrate, protein and fluid replacement.

The major sugar store is in the form of glycogen. This is made up of many repeating glucose units joined together, ready to be broken down to make energy. Repeated exercise will deplete these stores. After exercise the muscles are ready to be replenished. This is particularly so in the first two hours after the training session. Therefore, easily digested sources of carbohydrate should be consumed as soon as possible, often in the form of a sports drink or soft fruit. This should be followed by complex carbohydrates for the remainder of the two-hour period, such as a bowl of bran. Overall you should aim to replace 3gm glucose/kilogram of body weight.

Be cautious with protein supplements, because excess proteins are converted to fat. Protein also requires more water to be digested than carbohydrate or fat and this can lead to dehydration. A high protein intake can reduce calcium absorption. This may lead to a predisposition to a lack of mineralisation of bone causing stress fractures.

In general, a fast bowler who maintains an adequate total calorie intake of about 5,000 kilocalories (kcal) per day, of which 12 percent is made up of protein, will have sufficient intake to maintain the recommended 2g/kg intake per day. For a 70kg (11 stone) bowler in the strenuous conditioning phase this means 140g (5oz) per day. An average

120g ((4oz) chicken or turkey breast contains approximately 35g (1oz) protein.

If you want to gauge your fluid requirements you can develop the habit of weighing yourself before and after exercise. This can be done in varying conditions of heat and humidity. The difference in weight will be a good estimate of the amount of fluid lost during that session of training or actual play. Another practical method is to examine the colour of the urine each day. It should be clear to straw coloured and at least 900ml (1.5 pints) per day. As dehydration progresses, the urine will be of a darker colour and less in volume. Thirst is a poor indicator of the state of hydration – once you are thirsty it's too late, you are already dehydrated.

Try to consume fluids before, during and after exercise with the quantity determined by the above estimate. There are many different ready-made commercial varieties of differing flavours and tastes. Some fast bowlers make up their own solution of varying carbohydrate and sodium intake following field tests. Most sports drinks will contain carbohydrate concentrations of between 4 and 8 percent. Higher concentrations will slow emptying of the stomach and cause feelings of bloating.

Before the day's opening session, you should consider drinking 500ml (0.8 pints) of cold water 1–2 hours before the start of play. A further 600ml (1 pint) can be drunk in the last 15 minutes before opening the bowling. This may consist of a sports carbohydrate drink. During training lasting more than 60 minutes, or a day's play, you should attempt to replace half the weight lost, as estimated above, with cool fluids. Colder fluids are emptied faster from the stomach. A reasonable target is to consume 120–150ml (0.2–0.26 pints) per 20 minutes of vigorous activity. The rate will be less during a day's play, as the fluid replacement will be divided over a

longer time. Again this depends on ambient conditions.

After the period of exercise you should make up the remainder of the weight loss. It has been suggested that the use of caffeine helps to break down fat as a source of energy, thereby sparing the sugar stores in the body. It should also be remembered that caffeine strips nutrients from the muscles too. How great this effect is in a particular bowler will vary and there will be risks of heightened anxiety, increased heat production and dehydration. Similarly, alcohol consumption before and after exercise will cause dehydration. If caffeine is to be consumed, then it is imperative to ensure that rehydration has been achieved, lest performance be compromised. Alcohol, although calorie rich, does not contribute to the sugar stores in the muscles.

Therefore, to maintain adequate rehydration you should develop good habits in order to keep your wicket-taking performance at an optimum.

Variations on the Framework

If you don't want to stick to the suggested framework, you should try to achieve *at least* four sessions of aerobic activity a week for 45–60 minutes at a time, which is quite comfortable and does not leave you breathless. You should be able to carry on a conversation with someone whilst doing this form of exercise, which is a good checkpoint.

You can choose any form of exercise provided you work to the above parameters. The three most popular ways to achieve the desired effect are running, cycling or rowing. I was never a huge fan of running. I found it boring, but others don't mind and some love it. So choose an activity you prefer or perhaps try two or three different forms of exercise.

If you are starting out from a low level of fitness, you may find that working in

15-minute intervals and changing to another activity suits you best. To get started, the easiest way to exercise is to walk. You can achieve good aerobic results by walking. As you progress, you can power walk (rather than just amble along, which does you no good really), as long as you are working up a light-to-moderate sweat. When you feel able to, you can move forwards to other activities.

For an overall fitness workout, it's really hard to beat swimming. The water supports your body weight and there's virtually no impact on key joints. Again, make sure you're swimming at a level around the correct aerobic heart rate.

This type of cross-training activity where you exercise using different muscles is very helpful. If you *just* do one exercise the whole time, it only works those muscle groups for that activity. You can use other sports to supplement your activity schedules, and give you a relevant interest at the same time.

Aerobic capacity can be *increased* by maintaining the heart rate in the training zone of between 70 and 85 percent of the maximum heart rate for that individual. As you get fitter, your ability to stay in the aerobic zone will mean you can work at a higher heart rate and still have aerobic effects. For example, cross-country skiers can work quite happily at 80–90 percent of their VO_2 Max (the highest volume of oxygen a person can consume during exercise) at heart rates of 200bpm for three hours and still be mostly using aerobic energy systems. However, if I attempted this then I would not be very well in a short space of time, as my buffering capacity to mop up (or use) lactic acid will not be as developed. This is why you will need to determine your own levels.

These percentages are worked out after years of comparisons of heart rates and VO_2 Max obtained in physiology labs when examining athletes. From these tests, tables have been constructed that predict the potential aerobic capacity (VO_2 Max) for that person. If you want to find out more, your local, friendly trainer at a health club or gym will be able to help.

Regardless of the percentage of aerobic efficiency there always will be some *anaerobic* work going on.

Lactic acid is itself an intra-muscular fuel that only appears in blood tests done after exercise. This happens if an athlete is not 'fit' enough for his muscles to use it as an energy source. It stays in the blood because the liver cannot get rid of it. So rather than there being a switch from anaerobic to aerobic there may be a 'pyramid' effect of adding one system on to another. Don't get too hung up on it though. I'm simply pointing out how heart rates affect the type of benefits you gain. And it's only a guideline.

The maximum heart rate is estimated from subtracting the age of the fast bowler from 220. A twenty-year-old bowler will have a maximum predicted heart rate of 220–20, which equates to 200bpm. Therefore the aerobic training zone will be between 140 and 170bpm.

There are expensive heart-rate monitors that sound alarms around this 'training zone', but it is far simpler to measure the heart rate. This can be done by lightly pressing the wrist in the watchstrap area just to the outside of the visible tendons on the front of the wrist. You can count the number of beats in six seconds and multiply this by ten to give the number of beats per minute.

Alternatively, a tested and reliable method is to ask yourself how you are feeling during the training session. If the feeling is that of being somewhat uncomfortable then this correlates well with being 'in the zone'. The effect of this type of training will be to increase the density of the blood vessels in the muscles trained. Hence, more oxygen can be transported to them. Also, the muscles adapt to become more efficient at sparing sugar and burning fat preferentially during exercise. This increases stamina during the course of a start–stop day of fast bowling. Did you not realise how much a bit of huff and puff could help?

Interval training is essential in order to mimic the pattern of short sprints that a fast bowler performs. It involves short bursts of intense activity with periods of rest in between. The intensity has to be severe enough to build up lactic acid within the body. This form of exercise intends to build up the body's tolerance of lactic acid. The level of lactic acid produced correlates well with the intense discomfort experienced during this training.

A sports physician can measure the blood lactate during training sessions in order to plot the recovery rate of the lactic acid returning back to normal. In this way, results early in the conditioning phase can be compared to those later in the preparation phase, allowing anaerobic fitness to be plotted.

Because of the intensity of the exercise sessions, this type of training is quite likely to provoke injury and therefore should be supervised by an experienced coach or sports physician. So be careful – but it does have excellent results.

Weight Training

If fast bowling were all about strength alone, Arnold Schwarzenegger (apart from having one of the longest names in world cricket) would be the fastest bowler on the planet. Clearly, it isn't all about being as strong as an ox. In fact, many of the great, quick bowlers playing today, and in the past, have not been muscle-bound hulks.

However, a fast bowler's training programme should incorporate a strength-training component. Strength is *crucial* for bowling

success. The two primary reasons for this are to develop explosive power through the crease and to protect against injury.

Many bowlers totally neglect to develop explosive power. The reasons for this are varied. Some simply don't know how. Some have tried lifting weights and become injured (by doing the wrong kind of cricket weight training). Some don't think it's important, which is not true. In reality, to be a decent quick bowler, you'll need body strength to support the stresses you're put under by your bowling action.

In cricket training, whether a batsman, bowler or wicket keeper, it's the little things that add up to make a huge difference. If you add even a small increase in your power, your game can dramatically improve in all areas.

Here are some *general guidelines* for fast-bowling training:

1. Use a variety of weight-training methods, such as free weights, body weights, medicine ball, kettle bells (the kettle bell is a cast-iron weight that looks like a bowling ball with a handle attached) and surgical tubing exercises.
2. Avoid pressing movements with *heavy* weights (risky for the shoulder).
3. Train your lower body with heavier weights.
4. Train your upper body with lighter weights.
5. Never forget to train the core of the body (hips, buttocks, lower back).

Your aim with fast-bowling training is to build functional strength. Fast bowling is a discipline that requires you to stop, start, and explode. It's an activity dependent on explosive bursts of power, and reactions. You must train your body to be strong at a variety of angles and planes. Every bowler bends, twists, and releases the ball.

Medicine balls are an excellent fast bowler's training tool. A solid medicine-ball routine builds explosive power, and teaches your muscles to work together as one tightly knit unit. I'd start with an 8 or 9lb ball (3–4kg).

Here are a couple of suggestions:

- Find a place where you have a solid wall and about 3m (10ft) of ceiling height. Hold the medicine ball in both hands at chest height like a basketball player about to make a chest pass. At the same time, squat down and leap off the ground. Jump up in the air and push the ball up as high as you can against the wall. Quickly retrieve the ball and continue the drill for 30 seconds. See how many you can complete.

- Grab the medicine ball with your hands underneath. Squat down so that your thighs come parallel with the ground. (The ball is held with your arms dangling in front of your body. When you squat down, they almost touch the ground.) Leap up off the ground, and at the same time, thrust the ball up in the air. Do as many as you can in 30 seconds.

Both of the above drills will build incredible strength and power. They are excellent for fast-bowling training.

Weight-lifting routines for fast bowlers can be tricky. Many cricketers generally make the mistake of trying to lift too much weight with various overhead lifts. This can lead to a potential injury. If you can't bowl a cricket ball (or you can't bowl it very well), then you're not much use to your team. So, fast-bowling weight training should avoid any overhead lifts with heavy weights.

What do I recommend for your training?

Exercises such as the squat, dead lift and leg press are used for the lower body. Heavier weights are okay here, but get a spotter (someone who keeps an eye on you and is next to you as you do the lifts). Learn to do the lifts correctly. There are some other exercises you can do that will really make a difference, for example body-weight lunges (at different angles) and single-leg squats (these are very difficult). These two lower body exercises build excellent strength and flexibility in the core area, which is crucial for fast-bowling training.

Now your upper body. No fast-bowling conditioning programme would be complete without good old-fashioned push-ups. I know they're not high-tech, but they are excellent for cricket. They strengthen your shoulders and arms as well as your chest. They give you an awesome return on your 'sweat equity'. Try a wide variety and see if you can work up to a one-armed push-up. When you can do ten or so one-armed push-ups, then you're getting pretty strong.

Push-ups are an alternative to bench presses. But if you must bench press, only use dumbbells and avoid heavy weights. Again the risk of injury to the shoulder is ever present, especially with a barbell. So, if you're going to bench press, use dumbbells with a spotter.

Next, you need to do some chin-ups. Do them both with palms facing forward and towards you. These are difficult (most people can only do three or four), but again you get excellent return with this body-weight exercise.

Don't underestimate the value of body-weight exercises such as lunges, push-ups and chin-ups. Try them. You'll be amazed at what a regular, simple routine can do for you, and the risk of injury is minimal.

Alternatives to chin-ups are rows. Look for a machine that allows you to do them sitting down. Don't do lat pull-downs in front of your head (again, to avoid injury to your shoulders).

Kettle bells can be an excellent fast-bowling training device, particularly for the lower body. Kettle-bell swings build explosive power in the hips, buttocks and legs (not to mention stamina). These muscles generate the explosive power and speed you're after. Avoid overhead snatches and clean and jerks, but lower-body lifts and other core-area exercises are excellent.

Kettle bells are small and portable. You can take them anywhere, and can get a fantastic workout in just ten minutes. Kettle bells are the favourites of élite combat troops, and have been for some time. Many athletes are using them to gain an edge on the competition in their respective sports. Why shouldn't you?

Weight training should be undertaken in order to increase strength and power. The reasons for doing this are twofold. The greater the diameter of the musculo-tendinous unit, the greater the protection it offers against injury. Weight training is a key component in developing power. The improvement in this work done per unit time improves the explosiveness of the ball release as you exert maximal effort passing through the delivery stride.

Weight training is divided into isometric training, isotonic (not the drink) and isokinetic. Of these the most useful for the fast bowler is isotonic training. Isotonic training can be *concentric*, where the muscle shortens as it contracts to move a weight, or *eccentric,* where a muscle contracts as it lengthens.

Examples of isometric training include calf raise, bench press and dumbbell curl. Isometric contractions allow you to mimic the patterns of movement similar to those encountered in the bowling action. Therefore, the appropriate neural pathways and

muscle groups relevant to the explosive release of the ball will be conditioned. The improvement of training can be observed. This is graded according to the repetition maximum. The one repetition maximum (1RM) is the maximum weight that the cricketer can lift in one effort.

In such a session of training you will estimate the baseline weight to lift at 60–70 percent of the tested 1RM for that muscle group. You will then attempt to lift this weight a minimum of seven times, making up one set. This is the minimum number of lifts required to activate all the different nerve pathways from the brain to develop that particular movement pattern. You can repeat the number of sets two to three times with rest in between.

For optimal gains in the conditioning phase of training, the training should be done three times a week. Isotonic weight training is done on machines such as the Nautilus, familiar to many of us in the gymnasium, or with free weights.

With either of these there is the potential for injury. It is important when starting these programmes of conditioning that you are instructed by a qualified instructor. When attempting heavier weights later, it is sensible to have a 'spotter' present who can step in, should there be a risk of injury. The best place to do all this is at the gym.

Plyometrics

After you have developed minimal strength levels, plyometric training will be used to develop your explosive power.

There are rapidly executed consecutive movements that utilise the elastic components within the musculo-tendinous unit. The movements consist of an eccentric muscle contraction followed rapidly by concentric muscle contraction.

115

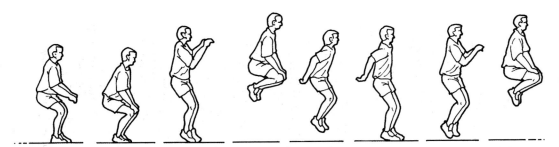

Repeated tuck jumps

Repeated long jumps

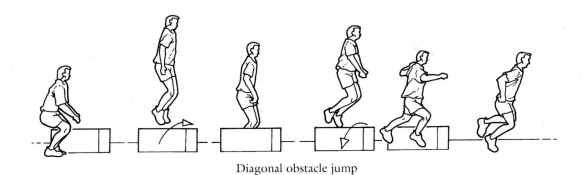

Diagonal obstacle jump

A series of plyometric exercises you can do on your own and without specialised equipment. The secret of exercising is being creative and making it interesting.

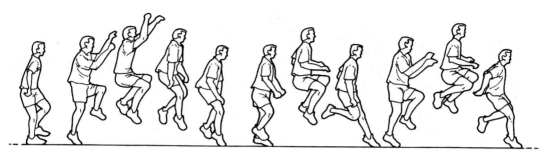

Alternate leg bounding

Squat jump

Power skipping

Single leg hops

The exercises comprise hops and bounds with as little time as possible spent in contact with the ground. Improvements can be measured by a sports physician using the standardised Bosco Jump Test. This involves timing the maximal number of jumps executed over a set time. A mathematical formula is then used to calculate a score of power developed. It is useful if not exciting.

Again there is the potential of injury and the programme will be developed in tandem with an experienced coach. You should report any soreness afterwards. This type of exercise should only be performed once or twice a week, when you are fresh, and further attempts stopped as soon as technique deteriorates.

Stretching

The purpose of this is to enable you to allow your arms and legs to move through an arc of movement without any hindrance.

In allowing a greater range of motion for the arm, for example, the limb can be accelerated for longer, allowing greater velocity at the point of releasing the ball. This is important if you're going to break the stumps when you bowl.

This means that greater forces will be generated and this may put the cricketer at risk of injury. Therefore it is critical to perform weight training in tandem with the specific purpose of increasing strength in this increased range of motion.

Whether stretching immediately before exercise helps prevent injury for that exercise session still remains controversial. Often stretching is included as a warm-up routine. It may be that the physiology of the actual warm-up is the more important component in altering the visco-elasticity of the muscle. A warmed-up muscle absorbs force better, thereby protecting the attached tendons.

There's some evidence to suggest that regular stretching three times a day can help prevent lower-limb injuries if done regularly over the longer term. The effect of this may be of increasing muscle diameter and again its shock-absorbing effect.

There are three main types of stretching done by athletes: static, ballistic and the use of proprioceptive neuromuscular facilitation (PNF). You don't need to remember this but it is worth an amazing 1,000 points in a game of Scrabble.

Ballistic stretching involves stretching to near the limit of the muscle and then performing bouncing movements. Unfortunately this rapid, alternating, stretch and relaxation can cause strong contractions in the muscle, with the potential for developing micro-tears. So be *very* careful with bouncing in a stretch. Do it only under the supervision of a qualified trainer.

PNF makes use of the fact that a muscle stretches more just after it has performed a contraction and also that it relaxes if its counterbalancing muscle is active. For example, when the biceps are active the triceps relax and when the quadriceps in the thigh shortens the hamstrings relax and lengthen.

This form of flexibility training is usually supervised by a coach or physiotherapist, as there is a tendency to over-stretch. Static stretches are the safest and most common type of stretches seen. The stretch position is assumed slowly without tension and the position held for 30–60 seconds. You should not experience any pain or discomfort in this position. In fact, you should feel the muscle gradually relax. It's a great stretch. And one of those moments where you think you're at maximum and the muscle eases off so you can go a bit further without forcing it.

The stretch is increased very gently to a new point of tension, even if this means only by a few millimetres. You will hold this new position for a further 30–60 seconds. Should you feel tension develop then ease back into the previous position. In the team setting it is natural to compare what the other cricketers are doing and be tempted into over-stretching. It is important to heed the feedback that one's own body is giving. Don't copy others. You are unique and flexibility and stretching are very personal things.

Speed and Agility Training

Your efficient and economical running speed to the popping crease is important in preventing fatigue and injury. As well as the above conditioning, coaches will supervise running drills that are aimed at improving the stride length and rhythm of the fast bowler. Such drills include 'high knees' and 'heel to buttock'. Over-speed work includes activities such as running downhill. Agility will be improved by running in a figure-of-eight pattern of variable diameters and stepping or hopping through patterns of hoops on the floor.

No one wants to be sluggish. Some are born with the attributes to run like the wind. Others are built more for chopping down trees. But as a fast bowler, you'll need to have a good basic speed across the ground and be at worst, decent in the field.

Cricket demands that cricketers are athletes and there is no greater athlete in a cricket team than the fast bowler.

All cricketers want to run faster and with greater ease. Speed is a function of power and coordination. The more power you can generate to get you forward, the faster you will move from point A to point B. The more biomechanically correct you are, the smoother your movements will be, resulting in greater efficiency. It means the more efficient you are the less energy you use, which results in an increased ability to sustain faster speeds over longer distances.

In order to improve speed you need to pay attention to it. It takes years of focused training to improve the various physiologic systems that are required for running, as well as the psychological aspects required to be successful. Nothing replaces a carefully planned, progressive and systematic running programme to improve your running. Speed drills can enhance the development of power and improve your biomechanics. Speed drills and other exercises can improve the coordination of these two elements. They can also help reduce the chances of injury.

Some of the speed drills and exercises that can help your fast-bowling performance dramatically are shown on the following page. There are many more not listed here. Some drills are best explained through demonstration. Speed drills will only help if you are diligent in doing them. They can be used as part of a warm-up, cool-down or as a specific workout. In general, they are listed from the easiest to the more difficult.

Naturally, some of these exercises are of the dynamic–plyometric type, therefore caution is advised. It is best to include a few of them very gradually at first. Start by doing a lower number of repetitions of just a few of the drills and then gradually build up to more repetitions. Eventually add more of the drills to your daily routine. Make it a habit to include some of these during every one of your workouts.

Not included here is a discussion or description of basic stretching exercises that should be done once the body temperature has been raised. Static or active isolation (AI) stretching exercises can be incorporated in between some of the speed drills or following them.

Also not included here is a discussion of other training strategies to improve speed and economy (the running programme, weight training, other cross-training activities).

Front lunge – feet together, hands on hips, step forward with one foot while bending the knee until in a lunging position and opposite knee is 15–22cm (6–9in) off the ground. Push off the front foot and return to feet-together position. The degree of effort can be varied by the amount of force you use to go forward and back. Repeat with other leg. Try 5–10 per leg.

Side lunge – feet together, hands on hips, step sidewards approximately 60cm (2ft) with one foot while bending the knee until in a lunging position. Repeat with other leg. Try 5–10 per leg.

Step-ups – on a step or bench. Step up with one leg, follow with other leg. Step down with one, and so on. You can add reps and eventually weights. The step should not be too high.

Two-legged jumps – like a broad jump. This is an explosive dynamic movement. Do one jump at a time to begin with. After you have done these for a while, start doing several in a row to activate the rebound action. Over time it will look like a frog jumping quickly. Build up to this stage carefully.

One-legged jumps – as above, but on one leg. This is more advanced in certain ways since you are putting all the forces into one leg instead of two. Short little jumps, flicking the ankle is what is desired and is the eventual goal. For starters, little forward progress is needed. Much later you can try a dash across 20–40m (21–43yd) for speed doing this.

Mogul jumps – Again, in the beginning, do very small lateral/forward jumps with feet together. These can be done one at a time or in multiples like a slalom skier.

Stork stand – stand on one foot – grab knee to chest. Hold position and maintain balance with either your foot held out in front of you

Front lunge.

Side lunge.

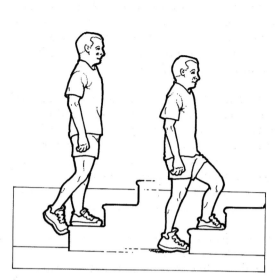

Step-ups

Mogul jumps. Use a fixed bar or rail for stability and support. Can also be done in the swimming pool whilst holding on to the side. Ankle weights are an option to increase difficulty.

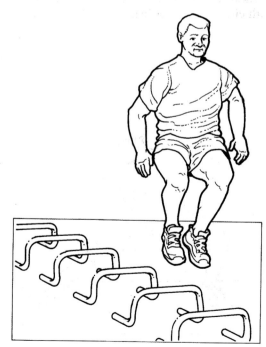

Double-leg jumps.

Single-leg jumps.

(you'll look like the Karate Kid) or with bent knee of to the side as in the illustration. Both ways are a great ankle and balancing exercise.

Running Drills

Fast feet – can be done while running or standing in place. On your toes, tap the front portion of your feet in running motion to the ground as fast as possible. Do not lift your feet more than 2–5cm (1–2in) off the ground. Start with three sets of 5 seconds and gradually build up.

Fast-feet ladder drill – with markings on the ground (socks, paper, slats of wood) place 10–15 markers about 38cm (15in) apart. With a running start run between the markers. Speed can be varied depending upon degree of knee lift. The shorter the knee lifts the faster the pace.

Skipping drills – basic skipping can be done in slow motion (walking) or at a faster speed. There are many variations that can be done, such as explosive knee-up lift, block-ing of the thigh, short hop on opposite foot, snap foot down to ground in flexed position, repeat with other foot. This can be a slow, forward-moving drill or have various speeds and movements.

Bounding drill – a high skipping movement, bounding high in the air off one foot, opposite foot drives high to the sky. There are many variations of bounding drills that can be done. These are often done best on hills with moderate inclines.

Strides – speed mechanics drills (40–100m (43–109yd) repeats at about a one-mile race pace).

Running tall – focus on head straight, chest out, hips forward, tight tummy.

Heel recovery – focus on high heel recovery to the buttocks. This exercise will not only emphasise the height of the heel (close to the buttocks) but also the speed of getting it there from the ground.

Recovery and block – focus on recovery of the thigh to the forward position and block the thigh in the upward position.

Pawing – focus on flexion of the foot upwards and snapping the foot down to make contact with the ground. Start with the focus on one foot. Try to alternate with every other step. Eventually do one side every step, alternating. Conclude with both sides pawing.

All together – focus on putting all the above together or combinations of them.

Remember to just add a few of these at a time – but do them regularly.

Stork stand.

Bowling Warm-Up

Not content with punishing you all-year round, fast bowling also requires important exercise prior to actually bowling in a match situation.

You'll find a minimal period of 20 minutes will be required for warm-up. Therefore your captain must alert the opening bowlers well before the start of play and those that are operating as the change of bowlers at least five overs before they will bowl. It doesn't happen that way because most captains don't think that far ahead. But that's the ideal.

There are many different warm-up protocols, all aimed at producing similar physiological and performance changes. They are aimed at lifting the baseline metabolism in anticipation of vigorous effort without depleting the energy stores in the muscles. The intensity will be at about 60 percent of the maximal aerobic capacity. This level of warm-up will produce mild sweating without fatigue. It can consist of jogging, callisthenics, stretches and mimicking the bowling action.

The effect of the warm-up lasts 30 minutes and has many benefits. It increases blood flow to the muscles that are active, the muscles and tendons warm up making them less likely to tear and rupture, the nerve impulses conduct more rapidly and there is increased oxygen release from the blood to the muscles.

Now you know the *official* reason why you should always warm up.

Pilates and Core Stability

Pilates is an excellent way to get the balanced core programme you'll need to support your bowling action. Apart from greater muscle tone and strength, Pilates offers you a unique combination of improved flexibility and core stability in the pelvic, stomach and hip areas of your body. This is vital to any fast bowler, as power comes from this area.

Core stability provides central body control, and allows you to generate power by maximising the efficiency of your muscular effort. Earlier in the book I talked about power being generated from the abs, stomach and hips. Well, core stability is the foundation for explosive movements and control (agility, balance and co-ordination), qualities vital in cricket.

Buy a Pilates book or get a video/DVD and exercise in your own home. If you have access to classes at a health club or sports centre, join one. Or you can use the Internet to find great examples of Pilates for all levels of student. Pilates is also very popular when combined with using a Swiss Ball (a large inflatable plastic ball that helps take the body weight).

Pilates can improve the ability of your trunk to support the effort and forces from your arms and legs, so that muscles and joints can perform in their safest, strongest and most effective positions.

In cricket terms, you become more stable in contact with the crease, better able to have a strong base from which to deliver the ball, and powerful in your ability to release the ball from your action.

By training specifically for core stability, you gain a number of benefits:

- Greater capacity for speed generation.
- More efficient use of muscle power.
- Decreased injury risk.
- Increased ability to be flexible in your body movement, as body momentum is controlled.
- Improved balance and muscular co-ordination.
- Improved posture.

A fundamental component of core stability and core-stability training is allowing your muscles to perform efficiently and reducing your risk of injury.

Yoga

You might be surprised to find that yoga makes a perfect companion for all cricketers but more specifically, for fast bowlers. In fact, most professional clubs now incorporate yoga into their important training routines. That's because yoga can help you develop a far better breathing technique while improving your balance, flexibility, core strength, and endurance.

The understanding of how to maximise the physical aspect of a fast bowler's make-up has brought us to an interesting area. The gentle, slow movements of yoga are ideal to complement highly energetic activities. And if you

A sample of Pilates exercises. There are hundreds.

think yoga is easy, think again. You require an amazing blend of control and patience when doing it. Plus, it has a genuinely mental aspect that helps with concentration.

Benefits of yoga for fast bowlers:

1. **Develop Deep, Relaxed Breathing**

   If you participate competitively in sport or simply join the occasional fun run on a whim, you are aware of the impact breathing can have on performance. Deep, relaxed breathing is the foundation of reducing performance anxiety and improving concentration. Yoga will help you develop a habit of breathing correctly. Yoga practice integrates the mind–body connection, and fast bowlers can benefit from this combination of skills training.

2. **Increase Core Strength**

   Yoga poses are all about building core strength. The slow, focused movements require a strong mid-section. The isometric contractions of many exercises will add a new form of resistance training to your typical machine-based workouts.

3. **Increase Flexibility and Range of Motion**

   Yoga routines incorporate slow, steady flexibility exercise that is ideal for fast bowlers. Frequent yoga training may increase flexibility and range of motion while relieving muscle tension. Improved range of motion can often help improve performance.

4. **Improve Balance**

   Yoga is a perfect way to incorporate balance exercises into your training routine. Balance exercises are often overlooked by fast bowlers yet are one of the most effective ways to correct muscle imbalance or body mechanic problems. With most sports and weight-training routines you tend to perform repetitive motions that develop some muscle groups while others are ignored. Yoga can fix these imbalances.

5. **Great Cross Training**

   Yoga is a great low-impact way to cross train. Cross training is necessary for bowlers who do the same routine all year round. Adding new exercises can help reduce injury, relieve training boredom, add variety and help recovery from hard aerobic or strength workouts. Yoga can be done at a high or low intensity and there are hundreds of postures that can provide a workout for your needs.

6. **Something for Everyone**

   There are many styles of yoga that range from very dynamic, active, movements that go from one posture to another (and result in a thorough aerobic workout) to more slow-paced practices that hold postures for several minutes and form an intense strength-training and balance workout.

CHAPTER 20

Making the Most of What You've Got

As we have now identified, your success as a fast bowler will be due to a combination of many factors, both physical and mental, that can be affected by the levels of understanding and practice.

To any young or aspiring fast bowler I say the most important thing is to enjoy the sheer thrill of bowling fast. It's a combination of excitement and expectation when you take the new ball – a feeling any true quickie will relish.

Irrespective of the level you play there's great fun and camaraderie in cricket. I would urge you to compete hard, try your best at all times and then enjoy the after-match activities too. It's easy to forget that without an opposition, you can't play. That's why I say you should be respectful to players and umpires who are turning out for the exact same reasons as you – to enjoy a game of cricket. Why else bother?

Bowling fast is a tough and sometimes thankless business. You'll need to be durable and certainly have a base level of strength and fitness. But if you do well, you'll gain the respect of your peers. And if you become really good, you may even be feared by opposition teams. That's a very uplifting and ego-boosting position to be in, as well as being worth a few wickets before you start.

I urge you to get out and practice what you've read in this book. Master one thing at a time and move on to the next one. But don't worry if you can't quite grasp things first time out. The fact that you are even trying to make positive changes starts the process of change. That's the mystery about improving.

And finally, experiment. If you don't try you'll never fly, so be open to the possibilities. The process of learning and improvement involves making mistakes. Have fun and above all be positive. When you're open to possibilities you're coachable and when you're coachable, anything's possible. If you do this, you'll already be way ahead of most other bowlers. I hope to see you at the top.

Best wishes
Ian Pont

Index